AQUAPONICS

4 Easy and Affordable Ways to Build Your Own Aquaponic System and Grow Vegetables All-Year-Round

RICHARD BRAY

Published by *Monkey Publishing*

Edited by *Lily Marlene Booth*

Cover Design by *Diogo Lando*

Cover Image by *Allahfoto/Shutterstock.com*

Printed by *Amazon*

ISBN (Print): 9798718844924
ASIN (eBook): B082GFYZ82

1st Edition, published in 2020

© 2020 by Monkey Publishing

Monkey Publishing

Lerchenstrasse 111

22767 Hamburg

Germany

All rights reserved, including the right to reproduce this book or portions thereof in any form whatsoever except for brief quotations in critical reviews or articles, without the prior written permission of the publisher.

MONKEY PUBLISHING

OUR HAND-PICKED BOOK SELECTION **FOR YOU.**

LEARN
SOMETHING NEW EVERYDAY.

Content

Introduction 5
    History of Aquaponics 6
    Hydroponics 8
    Aquaculture 10
Before You Begin 15
    Planning 15
    Goals 18
    The Basic Components 20
    Aquaponic Systems 27
    System Limitations 34
Plant Selection & Culture 38
    Basic Plant Care 53
Fish Selection & Culture 58
    Fish Culture 66
    Feeding 68
    Cycling 68
Nitrification, Mineralization, & Oxygenation 73
    Nitrification 74
    Mineralization 82
    Oxygenation 88
Media-Filled Bed 90

Building a Media-Filled Bed System 105
    10-Gallon Tank 106
    Stacked Tanks 113
    IBC Totes 124
Deep-Water Culture System 140
Building a DWC System 150
    DWC IBC Tote System 151
Maintenance & Troubleshooting 167
    Maintenance 168
    Troubleshooting 172
About the Author 180

Introduction

Aquaponics is a sustainable production system for both freshwater fish and a variety of plants. This system combines aquaculture and hydroponics into a symbiotic operation that produces over twelve times more plant material per square foot than traditional agriculture.

Aquaponics was rediscovered in the 1970s, and has grown into the frontrunner for sustainable food production now and into the future. While hydroponics and aquaculture are well-established production methods with large amounts of research, aquaponics is a fairly new field of study.

bluedog studio/Shutterstock.com

History of Aquaponics

Dr. Mark McMurtry and Dr. James Rakocy are credited with the development of modern aquaponics systems. In 1969, McMurtry began exploring how to integrate growing practices together into mutually-beneficial relationships at his own New Alchemy Institute, while Rakocy created a small aquaponics system as his Doctor's work at Auburn University.

Both men contributed to our modern aquaponics systems, with Rakocy and his colleagues developing the first commercial-sized aquaponic raft system, which completely eliminated the need for a grow media.

While these men are largely responsible for the aquaponics systems we use today, the concept of using fish and plants together in one production model is centuries old.

In the 15th century, the Aztecs created artificial floating islands called *chinampas* that resemble our modern raft system. The city of Tenochtitlán was the center of Aztec culture. It was located in the middle of a large lake, with surrounding cities built on the shoreline.

Due to a shortage of farmland, the Aztec people created a production method that used floating islands, chinampas, as a way to both grow crops and dispose of the city's waste water. They built large rafts and filled them with soil, then planted crops and flowers and anchored the rafts in shallow water.

Later, the floating raft system was replaced with permanent structures built in the marshy lake beds. Fences built with mud and branches were constructed to reach 10' in width and almost 3,000' in length.

Rows were constructed parallel to each other with canals of moving water running between them. This kept the crops irrigated, and also gave fish and waterfowl a constant source of food.

Nearly 1,000 years before the Aztecs built chinampas; Chinese agriculture had developed a similar system for irrigating and fertilizing rice paddies. Peking ducks kept on the water provided waste that the fish used for food. The waste from the fish provided the rice with essential nutrients, and the ducks ate the insects that were attracted by the rice paddies.

This system produced three products: rice, fish, and ducks. Each was a source of food, and each sustained the others.

Both systems serve as an example of sustainable food production. We can use the same concepts and techniques as we combine horticulture and aquaculture into productive home-based sources of organic meat and vegetables.

Hydroponics

Nattawud Groodngoen/Shutterstock.com

Many of the principles of a successful hydroponic system correlate to a successful aquaponic system.

Hydroponics is a production method where plants are grown in water, either on floating rafts or in soilless media. The necessary nutrients are supplemented with fertilizers, and the water is aerated to provide enough oxygen for the roots to function properly.

The most important factors when operating a hydroponic system are:

- Temperature
- Light

- Nutrients
- pH
- Water quality
- Grow media
- Cleanliness

Hydroponic systems can yield up to twelve times the amount of produce as traditional agriculture, but they do take more energy to maintain. Consistent tracking of temperature, pH, and nutrient content are imperative for a healthy system.

Pipes and fittings need to be examined on a regular basis to make sure algae growth has not clogged emitters and that there are no leaks. Ventilation and lighting need to be maintained to avoid pests and diseases, and the entire operation may need a greenhouse depending on the climate zone.

While hydroponic systems do take more work, the harvesting and planting process is much easier than traditional agriculture. There is no need to weed, which means there's also no need for harmful herbicides. Plants are grown at waist-height, which makes it much easier to physically monitor them. A closed system allows more control over the environment, and it's possible to formulate the exact nutrient requirements of each crop for maximum yield.

Overall, hydroponic systems are an incredibly high-yield production method, and it has made urban farming a viable source of fresh produce.

However, hydroponic systems don't generate their own nutrients, which is what makes it a perfect pair with aquaculture.

Aquaculture

Mati Nitibhon/Shutterstock.com

Aquaculture is simply the farming of aquatic animals for food. Marine aquaculture is the breeding and harvesting of marine animals; anything from oysters and seaweed to yellowtail and giant perch. Freshwater aquaculture farms catfish, bass, trout, and other fish in man-made ponds and lakes.

Aquaculture is a large industry, and aquaponics is not truly a merging of hydroponics and aquaculture. Rather, it is a mixture of hydroponics and recirculating freshwater finfish aquaculture, although some systems incorporate crawfish and mussels.

Salt kills plants, so this eliminates all marine aquaculture species from possible uses in aquaponics.

The most important factors in freshwater finfish aquaculture systems are:

- Temperature
- Light
- Water quality
- Feed quality
- pH
- Waste management

Hobby-sized aquaculture is quite simple; dig a pond, fill it with water, and add fish. There are some containment methods that make harvest easier, but most freshwater aquaculture systems use ponds for growing fish, and only use tanks for breeding purposes.

Aquaponics combines the *concepts* of hydroponics and aquaculture, but not necessarily the methods. Practically speaking, aquaponics is adding fish *into* a hydroponic system. Fish replace the need for synthetic fertilizers, but also make the process more difficult to maintain.

A positive byproduct is harvesting the fish, but the main focus is growing nutritious produce. Therefore, most aquaponic systems and research focuses on how to keep the fish happy enough to supply nutrition for plant growth.

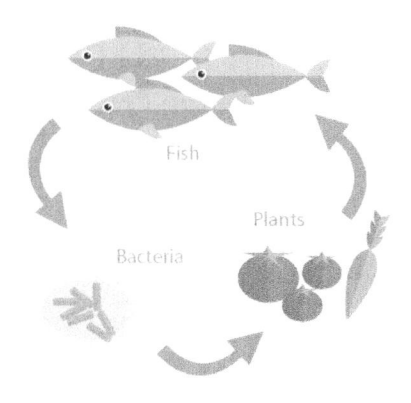

Konrad Mostert/Shutterstock.com

Pros & Cons

Maintaining an aquaponic system can be time-consuming, but it's simple once you understand the science behind a balanced ecosystem. It's best-suited for vegetable and herb production in a setting where the temperature can be easily controlled. Harvesting fish is a byproduct of a healthy system, and falls far short of the amount of plant material that will be harvested.

Pros	Hydroponics	Aquaculture	Aquaponics
High-yield plant production	X		X
Source of freshwater fish		X	X
Easy to monitor	X		X
Year-round production	X		X

Cons	Hydroponics	Aquaculture	Aquaponics
Frequent water tests	X		X
Seasonal harvest		X	
Constant temperature monitoring		X	X
Potential system failure	X		X

Aquaponics combines the benefits of both hydroponics and aquaculture, which also compounds the unique needs of each system. For example, pH is a key factor in both aquaculture and hydroponics, and both systems need to stay within a certain range for healthy development. However, plants need a slightly acidic pH of 6-6.8, while fish prefer a slightly alkaline range of 7-8.

Both are easy to maintain separately, but when you combine fish and vegetable production into one system, the target pH range becomes smaller. Most systems should aim for a pH near neutral for healthy fish, plants, *and* the bacteria that makes their beneficial relationship possible. Temperature, light, water quality, nutrient levels, and other factors have similar maintenance requirements.

Furthermore, some benefits of an aquaponic system may be cons for hobby growers. For example, year-round harvest means year-round maintenance. Luckily, the daily maintenance on an aquaponic system is simple; feed the fish and check the water temperature.

However, a successful aquaponic system can produce a large amount of fresh, organic produce. In fact, most systems are so productive that growers end up selling produce to neighbors, setting up community-supported agriculture organizations, or selling at local farmer's markets. A medium to large-scale hobby operation can serve as a decent source of side income.

The purpose of this book is to focus on hobby-sized aquaponic systems. These can range from educational 10-gallon fish tank systems to a full backyard of IBC totes. If you are interested in starting a commercial aquaponic operation, it is best to start small and learn the science behind maintaining a system before investing in expensive equipment. This will allow you to discover what is profitable in your area, if the fish and plants you choose are viable for the climate, and if you enjoy the process.

The first decision you will need to make as a hobby grower is where you will put your system. This will determine the temperature and lighting conditions, which will determine what plants you can grow and what fish will do well in your system. Once you have a location, you can begin the planning process.

Before You Begin

Aquaponics is a delicate balance of ecosystems. While it is commonly described as a system where the fish feed the plants, that's not really the case. Fish feed the bacteria, who then feed the plants.

Proper planning and design are essential for a healthy system, and a healthy system is essential for a healthy harvest. Thorough initial research will help you narrow down the best possible design for your location, which will lead to fewer costs and maintenance hours.

Planning

Before you build your system, you need to determine the purpose of your system. There are 3 common reasons for building an aquaponic system:

- Education
- Personal Use
- Profit

Once you decide on your reason for building an aquaponic system, you can focus your goals on that purpose.

Education

Educational aquaponic systems can range from a 10-gallon fish tank to a 10,000-gallon fish tank. The purpose for an educational system also varies. A small tank in your living room may teach your child where plants come from, but a large system may serve to teach aspiring growers how to properly manage their own commercial operations.

Educational systems should ultimately teach something, so this type of system should be designed around the power of observation. Clear viewing panels into a fish tank, various examples of grow beds and media, and different plumbing structures can show students how systems work best.

For a simple classroom tank, a clear fish tank and a small, clear, plastic grow bed can illustrate the concept of sustainable growing, while allowing students to observe the fish, plants, roots, and water circulation.

Large systems can have one or multiple fish tanks with different species, a variety of grow beds, and easy-to-access plumbing fixtures. They should also have freshwater test kits and pH meters to learn routine maintenance, and for diagnosing problems.

Personal

Personal systems also have a range of uses and applications. These systems are usually smaller, and the growers are more budget conscious. Eating healthy, sustainable food is the driving force behind personal systems, but that only works if the system eventually pays for itself.

Personal systems should ultimately provide food directly for the grower, so this type of system should be designed around variety. If your goal is to eat fresh, healthy, home-grown herbs and vegetables, then you will probably want to do more than lettuce and basil. Each plant has a different nutrient profile, so you want to maximize the benefits of growing your own veggies by eating a variety of plants.

Variety, in aquaponics, generally means a reduced yield. However, even a reduced yield in aquaponics is higher than the average traditional vegetable garden. It's easier to tailor the temperature, pH, nutrient profile, lighting, etc., to one or two crops. It takes more planning and maintenance to grow a variety of crops, but many growers are able to grow a diverse garden with the right system design.

This is why most personal growers opt for media-filled beds. Media, like clay pebbles or river rock, provides a great buffer for your aquaponic system, and it provides the biological surface area that bacteria need to break down waste into nutrients. It also allows you to incorporate worms into your grow beds to help break down sludge and other waste that's hard to clean.

Media beds offer stability for larger, fruiting plants, and they also cut down on the number of filters you need to keep your system running.

Personal systems are the most difficult to establish, since the crops are based on the grower's preference. If this is your first attempt at an aquaponic system, allow your climate and location to determine your fish and plant selection for the first year. Once you are comfortable keeping a system running, look into changing your fish selection or adding in new crops for a challenge.

Profit

Profitable systems are generally larger than personal systems, but they are much easier to plan and build. There are more components, but the focus is on mass production of one or two crops, so the system can be custom-made to suit the needs of particular plant and fish species.

Profitable systems should ultimately provide income for the grower, so this type of system should be designed around efficiency. This generally means more upfront cost on labor-saving elements. For instance, deep-water channel (DWC) systems allow for quick transplanting and harvesting, as well as moving large amounts of plants to different grow beds if necessary. However, the extra filters needed to make this system work can add to the upfront costs.

Planning for these systems should include the capacity to expand, space for workers to maneuver, a processing and packaging station, and a basic market study. Your plant and fish species will be determined by your market, not your personal preference. You may hate tomatoes, but aquaponically-grown tomatoes may be a high-income crop in your area. Do some research before you commit to fish or plant selection.

Goals

Once you've determined whether your motivation is educational, personal, or profitable, it's time to plan the more specific purpose behind your system.

Outline your purpose for building your system by answering these questions:

Who am I building this system for?

Are you building it to educate yourself, or to educate others? Are you building it to feed yourself, or to feed others? Do you have to meet the expectations of someone else, or do you have complete control over the design?

What am I going to grow?

An educational system should either grow a variety to demonstrate how to grow multiple crops, or a solitary crop to demonstrate how to grow things commercially. A personal system is dependent on what you like to eat, and how much. Profitable systems should grow what the market wants to buy, but only within the scope of what is cost effective.

When will it need to be operating?

A system needs time to build up the necessary ecosystem that helps filter water and provide nutrients. Once that cycle is complete, you can begin actively growing fish and plants. At this point you have two choices: harvest the plants and fish at the same time, and shut down the system for a period of time, or keep restocking fish and plants to run the system continually.

Where will it be operating?

This needs to take all aspects of your location into account; start big, and then focus on your specific location. What climate zone are you in? Will your system be inside or outside? Will it be small or large? Will it be in full sun, part shade, or under artificial lights? Is it windy? Will you need to add a water heater during the winter months?

Why aquaponics?

Aquaponics is the most mentally-involved growing system. Physical labor is reduced to transplanting, testing the water, harvesting, and checking your fish, so it's one of the least demanding production methods on a physical level.

However, there are many different ways to grow your own produce. Why does an aquaponic system fulfill your growing needs more than a traditional garden or a hydroponic system? Determine what makes an aquaponic system the best solution for your growing goals.

Once you can answer these questions, you should have a well-rounded list of expectations that your system should meet. These expectations will help you design your system.

The Basic Components

Regardless of which system you decide to build, each aquaponic setup will have eight main components:

- Fish Tank
- Grow Bed
- Biological Filter
- Solids Filter
- Water
- Plumbing
- Fish
- Plants

5: Plants absorb nitrates from the water

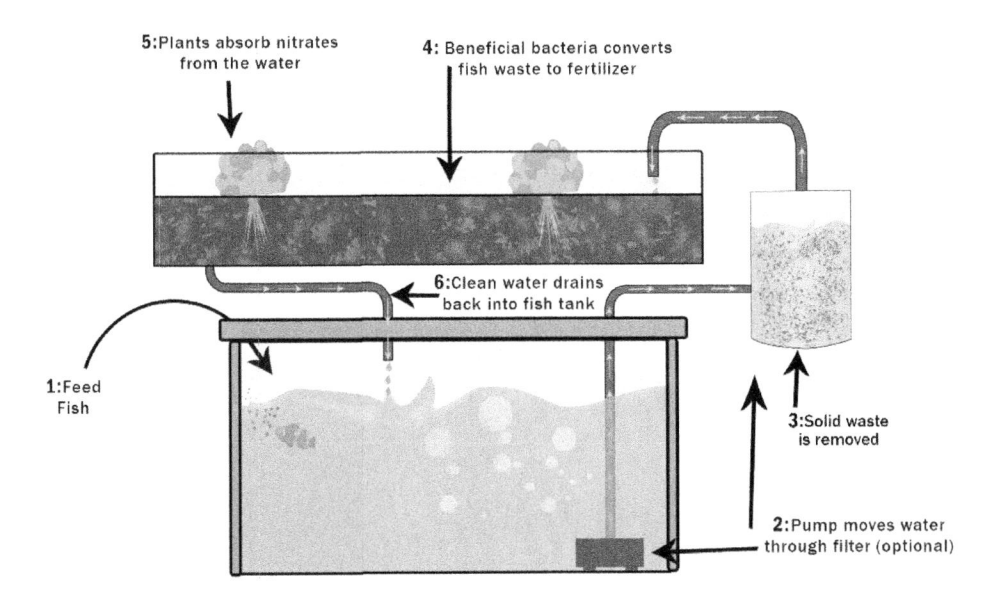

4: Beneficial bacteria converts fish waste to fertilizer

6: Clean water drains back into fish tank

1: Feed Fish

3: Solid waste is removed

2: Pump moves water through filter (optional)

Fish Tank

Fish tanks will have a similar design in all aquaponic systems. The only difference will be that large systems have large fish tanks, and smaller systems have smaller fish tanks.

A tank should value depth over diameter to help maintain consistent water temperatures. Deep, slimmer tanks lose or absorb less heat than shallow, wide tanks. However, the degree to which you value depth over diameter will depend on your fish selection.

Grow Bed

Grow beds are the most variable component in aquaponic systems, and they are generally what divides and defines the different systems. The grow bed is the part of the system that supports plant growth.

Media-filled grow beds are just that; grow beds full of media. These beds will be full of gravel, river rock, clay pebbles, lava rock, or custom media mixtures. Media helps to support taller plants, but the primary use of media is as a biological surface area. Pebbles and rocks give bacteria plenty of places to live and reproduce, which helps the bacteria filter waste from the water.

Pansim/Shutterstock.com

Deep-water culture (DWC) systems have beds without grow media, but may support plants in pots that are filled with media. These systems have less surface area for bacteria in the grow beds, but make up for it with the addition of a biological filter.

Hybrid systems are also defined by their grow bed design. Nutrient-film technique (NFT) beds are constructed with long rows of large PVC pipe with a thin film of water flowing through the bottom.

A-frames or towers are a way to organize NFT pipes to take advantage of vertical growing space. Dutch buckets mix the concept of a media bed with traditional drip irrigation, and drip nutrient-rich water into buckets full of grow media, which is then drained back out into the fish tank.

The purpose for your aquaponic system will help you determine which grow bed will work best for you. In general, the best hobby systems are simple stacked media beds or basic DWC designs with IBC totes.

Biological Filter

A biological filter does not catch or filter out visible waste. Its purpose is to filter out ammonia waste (urine) and convert it into nitrogen for plants; a process called nitrification, and to break down solid waste to convert it to other vitamins and nutrients; a process called mineralization.

Any surface area within a system can support the bacteria necessary for these processes, which is why biological filters are just a collection of small particles that increase the amount of available surface area.

These particles can be plastic balls, clay pebbles, rocks, plastic beads, or a number of other inert, small, or porous materials. In media-filled grow beds, the media acts as a biological filter. In all other systems, you must add a biological filter by plumbing in a tank full of media that allows the water to flow through on its way to the grow beds.

Solids Filter

A solids filter is meant to catch and filter out solid fish waste, excess feed, and dead plant material. Solids can be trapped in a biological filter, but the purpose of a solids filter is to remove visible waste.

Bacteria generally cannot keep up with the amount of waste that fish produce, and it would clog pipes and become toxic for fish if it kept recirculating through the system. A solids filter will help remove solids in a tank where they can settle and be easily removed from the system if there is too much buildup.

Water

Water is an obvious necessary component in an aquaponic system. Before you build your system, test your water. There are many additives in tap water, like chlorine, that can cause serious harm to your fish.

You should also test your water's pH, nutrient, mineral content, and salt content. A good rule of thumb is that if you won't drink your tap water, it's not suitable for aquaponics.

It's important to understand the properties of your water before you design your system, because it will influence your maintenance responsibilities. Part of regular maintenance on an aquaponic system is draining off a few gallons of water and replacing it with fresh water.

If your system runs at a pH of 7.2, but your tap water is 6.3, you need to adjust the pH so you don't shock your system. If your tap water has chlorine, you need to let it sit for at least 24 hours so the chlorine will dissipate. Many elements that are harmless for humans are detrimental to fish, so do an in-depth test on your source water before you build anything.

Plumbing

Puripatch Lokakalin/Shutterstock.com

Water requires plumbing, but luckily, the plumbing in an aquaponic system remains constant throughout the different designs. Water will need to be pumped, aerated, and filtered as it circulates through your system.

Water should be fully circulated through your system once per hour. This means if you have 1,000 gallons of water in your system, you need a pump that can handle at least 1,000 gallons per hour.

There is no such thing as too much aeration, so take advantage of every opportunity to agitate the water. Lack of oxygen results in anaerobic bacteria, which can cause a system crash. Electric aerators, manual aeration, and even biological filters can incorporate oxygen into your water.

Fish

Your fish selection will be determined by your crop selection and your climate. Any fish suitable for tank culture will work for aquaponics, although there are a few proven winners that are easiest in beginner systems. Fish are a secondary source of food and income in an aquaponic system. Plants will produce much more usable material than your fish tank, so plants are the priority crop.

Fish are cold-blooded, so their activity, metabolism, respiration, and movement depend on the water temperature. It is easier to heat water than it is to cool it, so pick a fish that can handle the warmth of your summer months, and add supplemental heating in the winter if necessary. You can cover your fish tank with a canopy and shade cloth to keep the temperature from fluctuating too much.

Plants

Plants are the priority crop in an aquaponic system. Plant selection will depend on the purpose of your system, but most herbs and vegetables are suitable for aquaponics.

Leafy greens, like lettuce, kale, and chard, do better in cooler systems with higher nitrogen content. Fruiting vegetables, like tomatoes and cucumbers, do better in warmer systems with higher overall nutrient content. A few fruits, like strawberries, will do well in an aquaponic system, although they are not suitable for beginners.

Indoor systems are susceptible to root rot and fungi, so make sure you can provide ample artificial light and ventilation. Large outdoor systems will be permanent, so find a sunny, level location. You can always cover your fish tank and grow beds with shade cloth if the water gets too warm.

Artificial lighting should be chosen based on the plants you will grow. Lights that give off heat, like halogen bulbs, should only be used for warm-season plants if you can justify the electricity usage. Otherwise, CFL is the best overall grow light.

Aquaponic Systems

All aquaponic systems have the same basic components, but they can be modified to fit a number of different growing scenarios. Each system serves a unique purpose, so before you decide which plants and fish you want to grow, research available system designs to see what would work best for your location. While any design can be scaled up or down for a hobby system, a basic media-filled bed or deep-water culture (DWC) system are best for beginners.

plants grow here
growing medium
clean water — **natural fertiliser**
fish swim here

AQUAPONICS

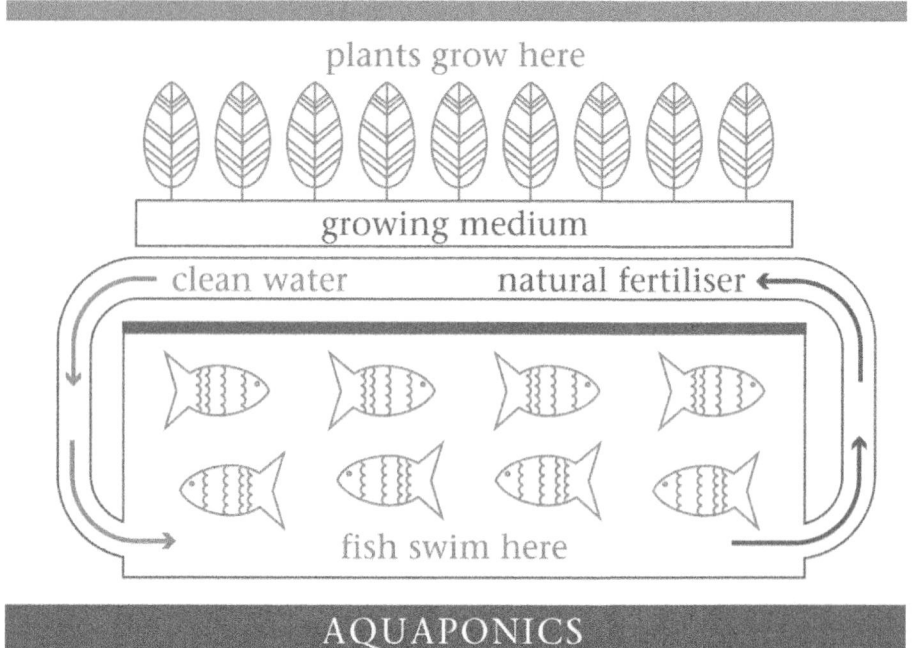

K-D-uk/Shutterstock.com

A basic aquaponic system consists of a fish tank, grow beds, and plumbing. Water is pumped from the fish tank into the grow beds, where plants are able to access nutrient-rich water. As the roots absorb nutrients, bacteria turn harmful fish waste into beneficial plant-soluble compounds. This process cleans the water, which is then returned to the fish tank.

Media-Filled Bed

This is the simplest system to build, and the easiest to maintain. Media-filled beds have a fish tank, solids filter, grow bed, and grow media. Many systems also incorporate a sump tank to help maintain consistent water levels.

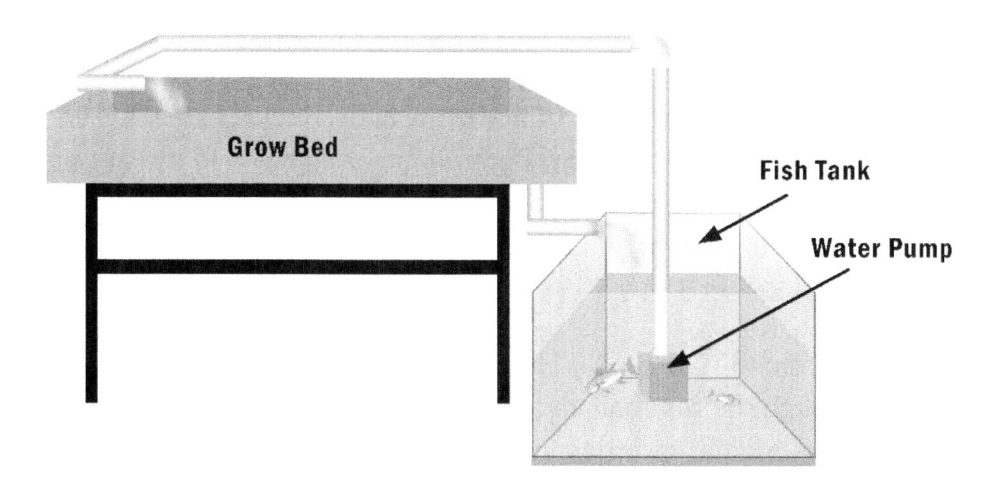

Basic media-filled bed systems consist of a grow bed with gravel or clay pebbles, and a siphon that returns water to the fish tank. Any design that fills the grow bed area with media, such as Dutch buckets, is a type of media-filled bed. However, when growers refer to a media bed system, they are generally referring to large, rectangular grow beds.

Most media-filled bed systems use a flood-and-drain circulation method. With this method, water is pumped from the fish tank into the grow beds once per hour, and allowed to drain back into the fish tank. This keeps roots moist, allows for nutrient uptake, but also prevents root rot.

Media beds help support plants, and act as a biological filter. They can also contain red wiggler worms to help break down organic matter and excrete worm castings, which are rich in nutrients. These beds support the most variety of plants and are easy to maintain.

Media beds are for small to medium operations, and it is best suited for personal or educational use.

Dutch Buckets

This system is a type of media-filled grow beds. Buckets are filled with media, and become small grow beds. Plants are placed in the top, and the buckets are lined up next to each other. Drip irrigation hose is laid across the buckets, and small emitters are aimed at the root ball of each plant

As water from the fish tank is circulated through the drip hose, it drips down through the root ball and into the grow media. As it flows down through the media, it settles in the bottom of the bucket. Hoses that connect each bucket together on the bottom drain the water back into the fish tank.

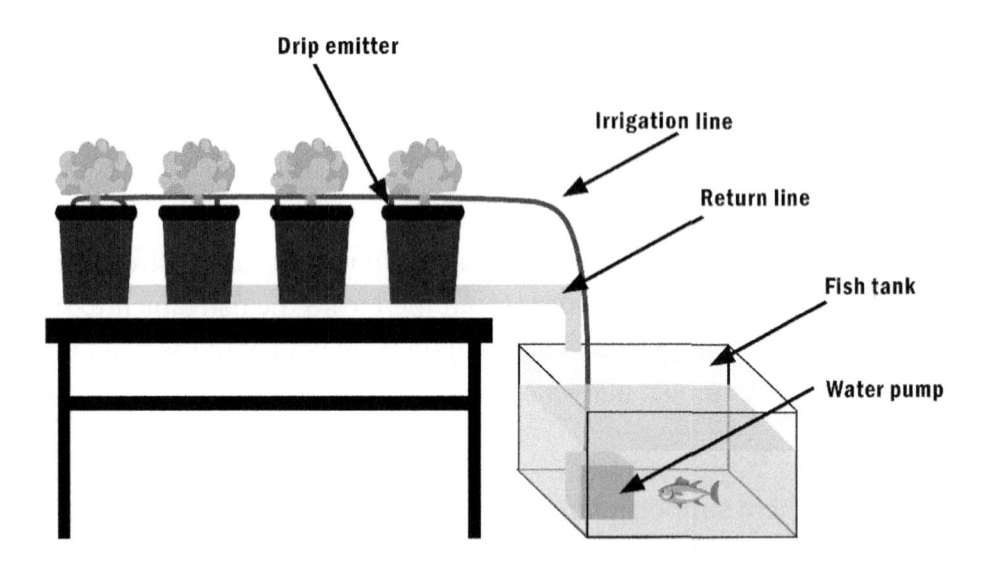

This system is perfect for large plants that are impossible to grow in other systems. However, these plants will also need supplemental fertilizers to keep up with demand.

Dutch bucket systems are best for growers who want to grow a specialty crop while conserving water. However, it will take more inputs into the system, and it may be harder to clean and maintain.

Barrelponics

This system is a type of media-filled beds. The only real difference is that every part of the system is made from barrels.

55-gallon plastic drums are used for the fish tanks, and then cut in half lengthwise to create the grow beds. One barrel is used as a solids filter, and another as a biological filter. The key to this system is to make sure your barrels were never used to contain hazardous materials.

The major benefit to this system is that it is easy to build frames and stack grow beds. The materials are cheaper, and they are easier to move than large IBC totes or stock tanks.

The major drawback is that the grow beds are too shallow for some fruiting vegetables, and you may need multiple fish tanks to hold the correct amount of fish. Barrelponics is a great option for growers on a budget who want to build an indoor system.

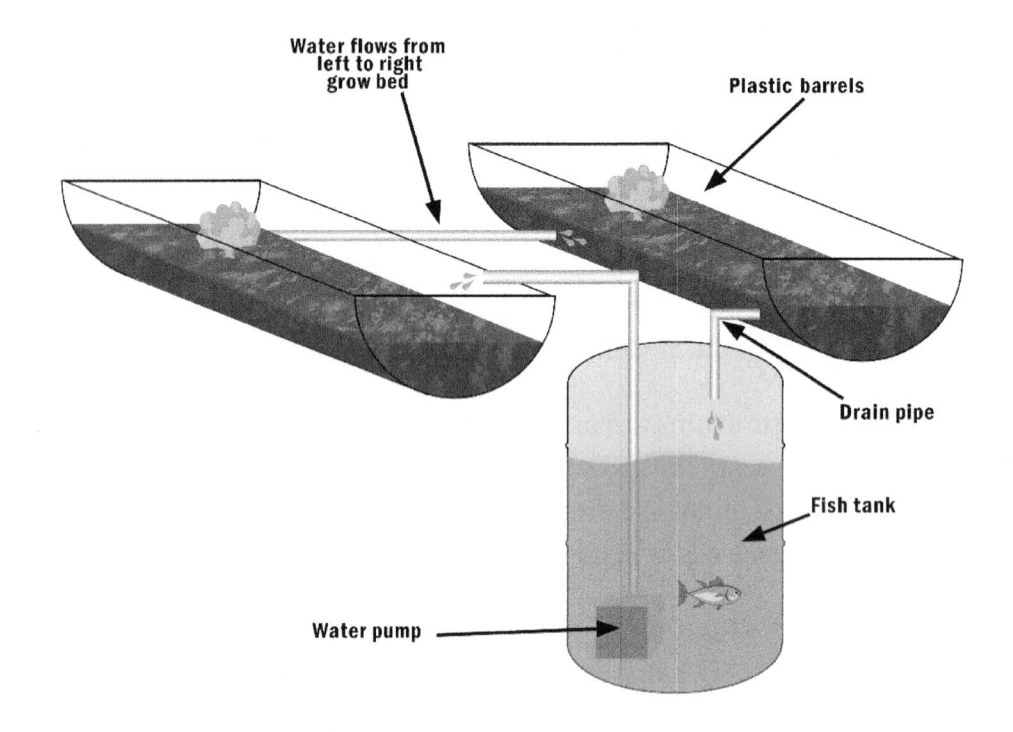

Deep-Water Culture

These systems are a little more complicated to build, because they need an additional biological filter due to the lack of grow media. However, they are easier to maneuver and work with on a larger scale, which is why this is the base system for most commercial operations.

Basic DWC systems use floats, rafts, or frames to suspend plants above the water in the grow beds or channels. Most DWC systems use a continual flow circulation method, where water is constantly pumped from the fish tank through the grow beds. Other types of channel systems, like the nutrient-film technique, suspend plants above the water in PVC pipe.

Plants may either be planted in rockwool or sponges directly into the system, or in a netted pot with grow media. However, the amount of grow media is small, meaning the system needs a biological filter for bacteria to filter the water and transform fish waste into nutrients.

DWC systems are best for medium to large operations, and are best suited for profitable or educational use.

Nutrient Film Technique

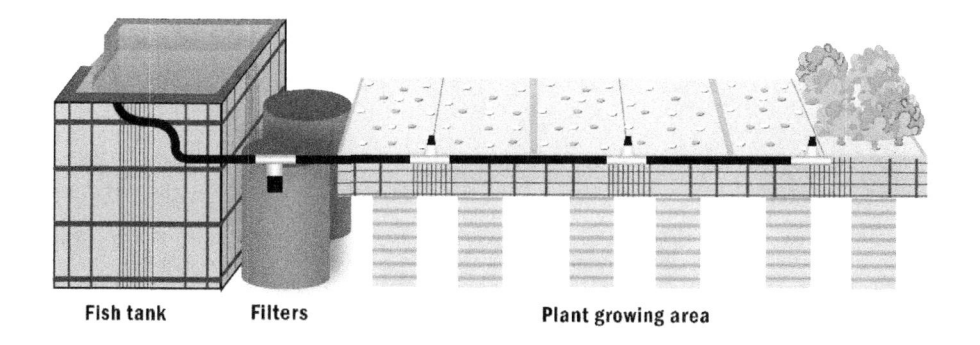

Nutrient-film technique is a type of channel system. Instead of large grow beds, like DWC, NFT uses PVC pipes laid on their side with holes cut on top for plants. Then, a thin film of water is circulated through the pipes, hence; nutrient film technique.

The upside to this system is that it conserves water and space. Pipes are lighter and easier to maneuver to take advantage of all available growing space, and they hold less water than traditional grow beds.

The downside to this system is that there is limited space for root growth, which narrows crop selection to leafy greens and some herbs.

However, this system is extremely efficient for large-scale growers who want to specialize in one or two leafy green crops.

NFT systems are best for large-scale, commercial growers who are planning to keep expanding their operation. These systems are not suitable for beginner, small-scale growers.

prapholl/Shutterstock.com

System Limitations

The final thing to consider before you build your system is potential limitations. Once you take stock of your limitations, you can plan the details of your system to maximize your production.

Climate

Unless you are willing to move, climate is a limitation you cannot change. Research which climate zone you are in, and the average cold and warm temperatures in your region.

If your system is going to be inside, then maintaining water temperature will be easier, but lighting will be more difficult. The opposite is true if your system is outside.

Climate zones are based on the amount of days each region spends below freezing. So, higher climate zones do not necessarily mean warmer summer weather.

Water is easier to heat than it is to cool, so if your summers are extremely warm, you may want to consider a canopy or other cover for your fish tank to keep the water from absorbing heat.

You can modify your climate by putting your system inside a greenhouse. A simple hoophouse will increase your growing climate by one zone, which can help maintain warmer temperatures during the winter. However, it will require ventilation during the summer to prevent overheating.

Indoor systems are prone to more diseases and pests if they don't have adequate lighting and ventilation. However, with proper light and air circulation, it is easier to grow year-round crops indoors because you aren't limited by winter weather.

Space

Your space limitations can help determine not only what kind of system you build, but whether or not you can meet your intended purpose. A profitable system will be difficult in a 4' x 6' backyard, and any system will be difficult in an area with full shade.

Measure the available space you have, considering light, temperature, and the ability to access and drain water. Figure out how much you want to produce, and how large your grow beds need to be. Then, figure out how large your tank needs to be to support your grow beds, how large your filters need to be, and where you will add supplemental lighting or ventilation.

Do not place 4' wide grow beds against a wall. The maximum width of a grow bed that is only accessible from one side should be 28", but it is better to keep them under 2' in width. This way, you are able to reach from one side to the other without crushing plants.

Finally, account for space to move around your system, check plumbing, test the water, move water, access your fish, start seedlings, transplant seedlings, and harvest mature plants. It is better to have too much work space than too little, since there is a considerable amount of maintenance required to keep these systems operating well.

Budget

Odds are, no matter what system you want to build, you do not want to lose money. This is especially true for personal and profitable systems, because the whole point is to either save or make money.

Aquaponic systems can be expensive, but many materials, like IBC totes, are easy to find for free. The most important factor for your materials is that they are food safe; don't use free materials that have been in contact with harmful chemicals.

There's also a monthly operating cost for fish feed, tests, amendments, and other materials. To get the most out of your system, grow higher-value crops, like tomatoes and peppers.

Time

Planning, designing, building, and operating an aquaponic system takes time. Most hobby growers choose aquaponics because it has higher yields and lower physical inputs than traditional gardens.

First, consider how much time you can devote on a weekly basis. Personal systems are generally easier to maintain because nobody else is depending on your harvest. Profitable systems, on the other hand, need to meet a continuous demand to fill orders or sell at farmer's markets. Educational systems will require time to train and educate students, plus routine maintenance.

Once you've established a routine, maintaining an aquaponic system is simple. Most of the work is water tests, feeding fish, adding water, transplanting, harvesting, and checking for clogs and buildup.

Aquaponic systems contain live animals, so you either have to find someone to feed your fish or purchase an automatic fish feeder if you are going to be gone for more than a day. Make sure you have a trusted helper to maintain your system when you're travelling.

Plant Selection & Culture

The varieties of plants and fish you choose for your system will be determined by a number of factors:

- Where the system is physically located (inside, outside, in a greenhouse, under a canopy, etc.).
- Where the system is geographically located (climate zones).
- Harvest goals (dynamic harvest for a family, or 2-3 crops for farmer's markets).
- Limitations (available space, available energy, cost, time, water quality, light, etc.).

You can either decide on which aquaponic system to use, and allow that to determine your plant and fish choice, or you can decide on your plants and fish, and allow that to determine your system.

In general, media-filled beds offer variety, while deep-channel systems offer quantity.

While it's possible to grow anything in an aquaponic system, the best beginner crops are herbs and vegetables.

Many produce items we consider to be vegetables are actually fruits. This distinction can help sort out why some plants do well in one system and struggle in another.

bayuuafif/Shutterstock.com

In the purest sense, vegetables do not even exist. They are merely a term used to denote a certain group of immature plant structures that are nutritious, edible, immature, and not particularly sweet. Celery is a stem, kale is a leaf, and a carrot is a root. These plant structures are edible at any point in a plant's life, but they are best when the plant is young. This is why baby versions and "micro" greens are so popular.

Why is this important? Because if an edible portion of a plant is *not* a fruit, then it requires less nutrition, time, and space to grow.

Peppers, tomatoes, cucumbers, peas, and other produce items with seeds are fruits. In order for a plant to produce fruit, it has to reach maturity. Then, it puts a large amount of energy and nutrition into forming a seed and a protective outer layer for that seed; the flesh that we eat.

In order for a plant to produce a fruit, it needs more time, light, space, and nutrition. Most fruiting plants also need a support structure, like cages or trellises. Squash and cucumbers will spread out over 10' unless they are tied up onto a vertical frame. These structures are difficult for a floating foam board to support without breaking or tipping over.

This is why media-filled beds are the primary choice for fruiting plants. The media offers a more permanent home for plants that need to reach maturity before producing, and it also holds more nutrition while allowing the roots to spread out over a large area. Deep-channel systems can support fruiting plants, but they need modifications, larger pots, additional nutrients, and more complex trellising.

The easiest way to grow fruiting vegetables in an aquaponic system is by planting dwarf varieties. There are dwarf pepper and eggplant varieties, bush peas and beans, and miniature melons and squash. Many varieties that do well in square-foot gardens, hydroponic systems, and container systems do well in an aquaponic setup.

Hybrid systems like Dutch buckets work well to support large, fruiting plants on a small scale, whereas NFT systems and vertical frames work well to support small, leafy vegetables on a large scale.

Plants	Media-Filled Beds	Deep-Water Culture
Lettuce/Arugula/Spinach/Mizuna	X	X
Herbs	X	X
Kale/Chard/Pak Choi	X	X
Peppers/Tomatoes	X	
Cucumbers/Squash/Melons	X	
Beans/Peas	X	
Broccoli/Cauliflower	X	
Houseplants/Flowers	X	X
Strawberries	X	X

Lettuce/Arugula/Spinach/Mizuna

- Water temperature: 65°-74°
- Air temperature: under 75° to prevent bolting
- Plant spacing: 7"-12"
- Germination time: 3-7 days
- Time to harvest: 25-40 days
- Compatible systems: All

Leafy greens are the easiest plant to grow in any aquaponic system. Loose-leaf lettuces are ready for harvest in about 40 days (earlier for baby greens), and head lettuces are ready in about 90 days. Arugula, spinach, and mizuna are all better when harvested young, and they can all be planted close together.

Salad greens do well in cooler conditions, and they can tolerate partial shade. This is helpful for indoor systems, because lettuce thrives under artificial lighting, and can handle cool environments, like basements.

Lettuce and other greens can be planted very close together as long as there is enough lighting. You can either harvest entire heads, or, in smaller systems, you can plant loose-leaf varieties and harvest a few leaves at a time.

Herbs

- Water temperature: 65°-70°
- Air temperature: under 75°
- Plant spacing: Varies
- Germination time: Varies
- Time to harvest: Varies
- Compatible systems: Flood-and-drain

Herbs are the second easiest plants to grow in aquaponics. They are also one of the most popular for hobby businesses who sell to local restaurants.

Most herbs prefer full sun, and need their roots to dry out periodically, which is why they perform best in flood-and-drain systems. In general, herbs with green, fleshy stems will do well in aquaponic systems. Herbs with brown, woody stems are more susceptible to root and stem rot.

Herbs that grow well in aquaponic systems are:

- Basil
- Parsley
- Oregano
- Anise
- Chives
- Cilantro
- Dill
- Oregano
- Thyme
- Lemon balm
- Marjoram
- Sage

Other herbs, like lavender, prefer drier growing conditions. They can be grown in an aquaponic system, but it will require more maintenance and monitoring to prevent rot.

These herbs include:

- Lavender
- Tarragon

- Rosemary
- Chamomile
- Echinacea

Mint grows exceptionally well in aquaponic systems, but it can quickly take over a grow bed. If you do want to grow mint, you should have a dedicated grow bed so it doesn't spread and choke out other plants.

Kale/Chard/Pak Choi

- Water temperature: 63°-70°
- Air temperature: 45°-75°
- Plant spacing: 18"
- Germination time: 4-7 days
- Time to harvest: 2-4 months
- Compatible systems: All

Dark, leafy greens like kale and Swiss chard are easy to grow in an aquaponic system. They tolerate a wide range of nutrient and pH values, and they have very few pest problems. Dark salad greens like cooler weather, and can tolerate light shade. Warm temperatures can cause leaves to taste bitter, and plants to grow long and leggy.

The roots of these plants are susceptible to rot if the water is too warm, so these greens pair well with cool-water fish.

Peppers/Tomatoes/Eggplant

- Water temperature: 65°-75°

- Air temperature: 55°-85°
- Plant spacing: 8"-2'
- Germination time: 10-21 days
- Time to harvest: 2-4 months
- Compatible systems: Media bed

Tomatoes, peppers, and eggplant are all members of the Solanaceae family, and are frequently listed as easy-to-grow hydroponic plants. However, adding fish into the equation makes it more difficult to maintain the amount of nutrition these plants require for fruiting.

It is much more difficult to supplement an aquaponic system with a nutrient solution, because the nutrients can have adverse effects on the fish. This is why it's easier to grow fruiting plants, like tomatoes, in growing media. The media holds onto bacteria that turn fish waste into nutrients, which gives the plant a more nutritious foundation.

Deep-channel systems can support plants in the Solanaceae family, but it will either require a higher stocking density or carefully-calculated supplements. Either system will need trellising to support heavy, fruiting branches.

If you want to grow tomatoes, you will want to decide if you are growing *determinate* or *indeterminate* varieties. Both have advantages in an aquaponic system.

Determinate varieties are more compact and bushy, and each branch terminates as soon as there is fruit set at the outermost bud. Indeterminate varieties are vining tomatoes, and they will continue growing and producing fruit until they are killed off by temperature changes. Determinate varieties are easier to grow in a media bed or

Dutch bucket system, while indeterminate varieties are easier to trellis and can be grown in DWC systems.

Plants in this family require warm temperatures to produce sweet fruit, so it's best to grow them outdoors during the summer season. This also makes them a good pair with warm-water fish.

Plants in the Solanaceae family are susceptible to many pests, including:

- Mosaic virus
- Blight
- Whiteflies
- Spider mites
- Blossom end rot
- Grey mold

Stressed plants are more susceptible to pests, so it's important to give them plenty of space to avoid branches rubbing together and creating open wounds. Adequate light is also important for plants to grow bushy and compact, instead of long and leggy.

Cucumbers/Squash/Melons

- Water temperature: 65°-75°
- Air temperature: 60°-80°
- Plant spacing: 1'-2'

- Germination time: 3-7 days
- Time to harvest: 2-3 months
- Compatible systems: Media bed, DWC

Fruiting vines are heavy feeders, and they need large amounts of nutrients for a flavorful product. They also need warm, well-lit growing conditions, and a sturdy trellising system to support heavy fruit.

Fruiting vines are water hogs, and once they begin producing, they can absorb large volumes of water. This will create juicy, full fruit, but without warm growing conditions and ample light, it will have a diluted, watery flavor.

Cucumbers can be grown in media beds and DWC, since they don't need to support the sugar content of melons, and they don't need to create large amounts of flesh like squash. Cucumbers are also easier to trellis because their fruit is smaller, and the vines are easier to control.

Melons and squash can be grown aquaponically, but they require more support and nutrition than cucumbers, so they are best in media beds. They produce heavy fruit that is difficult to trellis because the vines cannot support them. For personal beds, immature squash and melons can be put in pantyhose and tied up to support the weight of the growing fruit.

These plants are difficult to grow inside because they require insects for pollination. Each flower is either male *or* female, and the pollen must move from the male flower to the female flower via a pollinator in order to create fruit. If you are growing these plants inside, you can take a small paintbrush and gently brush the inside of each flower to distribute the pollen on the female flowers.

This process is simple for 1-2 plants, but it is too time consuming for large, indoor growing systems. Therefore, these vines should only be grown outdoors if you want to grow them on a larger scale. However, they are highly susceptible to cold weather, so a summer crop of vines should be replaced with crops that endure cold weather during the fall, winter, and spring.

Beans/Peas

- Water temperature: 65°-75°
- Air temperature: 60°-80°
- Plant spacing: 6"-12"
- Germination time: 7-14 days
- Time to harvest: 2-3 months
- Compatible systems: Media bed, DWC

Beans and peas are a perfect combination in an outdoor aquaponic system. Both require similar nutrition, lighting, and trellising. However, peas grow best in cooler weather, and beans grow best in warmer weather.

A system built to support peas can be planted early in the spring, and once the peas have finished producing, they can be replaced with beans during the warmer summer season. Peas can be planted again in the fall once the beans have stopped growing, and depending on your climate, these can be grown through the winter.

Peas perform better in indoor systems than beans primarily because peas prefer cooler weather and can tolerate some light shade. Peas and beans are self-pollinating, so they can produce fruit indoors without pollinating insects. However, placing a few fans around your system will aid the pollination process.

The most difficult part of growing peas and beans in an aquaponic system is that legumes naturally fix nitrogen into their substrate. Instead of pulling nitrogen from the water into the plant, the plant puts nitrogen back *into* the water. This can result in toxic levels of nitrogen for the fish unless there are other plants in the system that will utilize it.

If you are growing legumes in an aquaponic system, plant them near where the water comes into the grow beds. Plant nitrogen-loving plants towards the end of the grow bed, before the water circulates back to the fish tank. This will help the plants filter out excess nitrogen before the fish are exposed to it.

Broccoli/Cauliflower

- Water temperature: 60°-65°
- Air temperature: 55°-65°
- Plant spacing: 12"-16"
- Germination time: 7-14 days
- Time to harvest: 4-5 months
- Compatible systems: DWC, drip irrigation

These plants are members of the cole crops, and they are some of the hardest plants to grow in an aquaponic system. Broccoli and cauliflower are the flower structure of a plant, which means they are treated like other fruiting vegetables. However, high nitrogen levels can cause hollow stems which results in a poor-quality product.

Cole crops need a cooler growing environment, longer growing time, and a light source that does not produce heat. While they can be grown in a cooler, dedicated media bed, if they are grown with other plants in warmer conditions they will likely bolt and become bitter.

Media beds also hold onto more bacteria that provide more nutrients to plants. This can cause broccoli to grow too quickly, resulting in hollow stems and a bitter, tough product. Grow media can also harbor fungi, and plants in this family are particularly susceptible to fungi that attack the roots.

Overall, DWC systems provide the best growing conditions for broccoli and cabbage. However, the roots are susceptible to rot if they are constantly wet. The best system for growing these vegetables is a flood-and-drain, DWC system or a drip system with smooth river rock or gravel as a growing media.

Indoor systems provide better control over temperature, but it can also encourage more pest problems. There are many pests that attack cabbage and broccoli, including:

- Cabbage webworm
- Cabbage looper
- Cabbage aphids
- Cabbageworm
- Clubroot

Large-scale, for-profit production of aquaponic cole crops is extremely difficult without the ability to control water and air temperatures, and monitor root health. In a personal system, one or two plants should grow well if they are planted in the early spring and late fall. Pull any plants that show signs of disease before it spreads to other plants.

Houseplants/Flowers

- Water temperature: 65°-80°
- Air temperature: 60°-80°
- Plant spacing: Varies
- Germination time: Varies
- Time to harvest: Varies
- Compatible systems: All

Many houseplants can be propagated by a cutting, which makes them incredibly easy to grow in an aquaponic system. If you want to grow a large amount of houseplants for sale, this may be difficult, since you will need to transplant each plant into a pot for buyers. The aquaponic system would only serve as a propagation bed, and would add unnecessary time and cost to the final product.

Many flowers grow well in an aquaponic system, but it may be difficult to grow flowers for bouquets. Many popular cut flowers, like daisies, have tough, fibrous stems that help them last longer in an arrangement. However, plants with tough, fibrous stems generally like warm, dry conditions.

Plants with green, fleshy stems don't hold up as well in a flower arrangement, but they are the flowers that grow well in an aquaponic system. That's not to say you can't grow an incredible variety of flowers, but you may have difficulty finding buyers since your flowers will have a limited shelf life.

Strawberries

- Water temperature: 57°-70°
- Air temperature: 60°-80°
- Plant spacing: 6"
- Germination time: N/A
- Time to harvest: Varies
- Compatible systems: All

Strawberries are one of the only fruits suitable for beginner hobby growers. Most fruits require a lower pH than vegetables, which can make them difficult to balance in an aquaponic system.

Strawberries are not propagated by seed. Instead, stems, called *stolons*, are rooted in new pots or media to create new crowns. Strawberries are either June-bearing or everbearing. June-bearing strawberries will produce a large crop for a few weeks during the warm summer months. Ever-bearing strawberries produce a smaller number of fruits at one time, but the harvest season is longer.

Strawberries require warm temperatures for the fruit to sweeten, so outdoor systems may be easier to start an aquaponic strawberry patch. One consideration for strawberries in your system is that they are perennial, meaning they do not need to be replanted after each harvest. If you have space to dedicate to a permanent strawberry patch, aquaponic berries can be a wonderful addition to your grow beds.

Basic Plant Care

Regardless of which plants you decide to grow, they will all follow the same basic process of germination, transplanting, maturation, and harvest.

Germination

All vegetables can be started from seed. Some take longer than others, but starting plants from seed is an easy process.

It's important to start your own seeds instead of buying vegetable starts from a greenhouse. If you purchase vegetable starts, you will have to completely wash the soil off the roots before introducing them into your system. If you don't, you may introduce soil-borne pathogens into your system, and you may also throw the plant into shock. If a plant is raised in soil, and then introduced to a water-based growing system, it may not be able to handle the transition.

You also risk mixing pesticide and fertilizer residue into your aquaponic ecosystem if you use plants from a nursery. These may have little effect on the plants, but they can wreak havoc on your fish tank.

You will need the following equipment for germinating seeds:

- Vegetable seeds
- Inert seed-starting media

- Heat pad (for fruiting vegetables)
- Grow lights
- Humidity dome (optional)
- Spray bottle full of water

Rockwool and germination sponges are the most popular methods for starting seeds for an aquaponic system. Avoid any organic seed starting media, like coconut coir and peat pots, because it can throw off the ecosystem.

Soak seed-starting media until it is thoroughly saturated before planting seeds. This can take up to 24 hours for rockwool slabs. Allow the media to drain freely, without squeezing or wringing out excess water.

Place the moist media in a tray, with the small impressions facing up. Place 1-2 seeds in each impression, and cover the tray with a clear plastic humidity dome.

If you are planting warm-season crops, place the tray on a heating mat. If you are planting cool-season crops, you can put the tray in a well-lit, warm corner of your house.

Each day, remove the humidity dome for a few hours to prevent the seeds from molding. Spray any dry spots on the grow media. Once half of the seeds have sprouted, remove the dome. If you are starting seeds indoors, you will need a grow light as soon as the seeds start germinating. Use a light that does not give off heat, and place it a few inches above the seedlings.

Tamisclao/Shutterstock.com

Transplanting

After 2-3 weeks, seedlings will be ready to transplant into your aquaponic system.

If you are using a media-filled bed, you can plant the seedlings directly into the media as long as the roots are long enough to reach the water. If you are using netted pots with a soilless media, transplant the seedling into the pot, fill around it with the media, and place it into the system.

Drip systems and wick systems help seedlings transition easier, because they bring water up into the root zone. However, most seedlings will acclimate easily after they have a few sets of true leaves and a few inches of root growth.

Maturation

Once the seedlings are transplanted, they will stay in the aquaponic system until it is time for harvest.

During this time, it is important to maintain the correct water temperature, air temperature, light levels, and nutrient levels for your plants *and* fish. Keep a log of daily and weekly tests to learn how your system responds to adjustments and external forces.

Harvest

Most plants are able to be harvested within a few months of transplanting, and many can be harvested on an as-needed basis. Staggered planting dates will result in staggered harvest dates, which will result in a more consistent, reliable harvest over a longer period of time.

Plants go through two phases of photosynthesis; a light-dependent reaction during the day that creates ATP, and a light-independent reaction at night that creates carbohydrates. In general, the best time to harvest produce is early in the morning when the plant is transitioning out of the light-independent reaction.

During this time, the plant is full of water (turgid), and also sweeter. As a result, it has a longer shelf life and a crisp, sweet flavor.

Make sure you have seedlings ready to take the place of plants you pull out of the system. Pulling large amounts of plants from the system can throw off the ecosystem if they aren't replaced with new material.

Once you have chosen which plants you want to grow, you will know the basic growing conditions your system needs to maintain; primarily, water temperature. Most systems need to maintain 65°-80°, but this can vary depending on your crop. Water temperature will be one of the primary factors that determine which fish will thrive in your system.

Fish Selection & Culture

The fish in your system will provide the nutrients for your plants. This dynamic relationship between fish and plants can be difficult to maintain, which is why it's important to choose fish that are appropriate for your system, climate, and crop selection.

Foto-Sabine/Shutterstock.com

Any freshwater fish that does well in tank culture is a possible candidate for an aquaponic system. Fish must be stocked to a certain density ratio to achieve the right proportion of nutrients in the water, so any fish you choose must be able to thrive in close quarters.

There are two different ways to determine how much fish you need in your system.

If your goal is to maximize fish growth for harvest, you need a lower stocking density to give them space to grow to a full size. In general, this means using a 1:10 ratio of 1lb of fish weight to 10 gallons of tank water. Calculate the fish weight based on the average, mature weight of the fish.

If your goal is to maximize nutrient content in the water, you need a higher stocking density to create more waste for the system. This can range from 1:10-2:10 pounds of fish to gallons of water, depending on how well the fish can tolerate higher stocking densities.

However, stocking density is only part of the equation. Higher volumes of fish will only result in higher volumes of nutrients if the fish are fed the correct amount of food, and feeding rates depend on the age of the fish. Young fish can eat up to 30% of their body weight in food each day, and produce significantly more ammonia than adult fish. Adult fish eat much less, about 3% of their body weight, and produce less ammonia per pound of body weight.

The amount of fish your system can support will also depend on your grow bed area. For every 1lb of fish, you need 50 sq' of biological filter surface area. This includes the surface area of your grow bed, grow media, filters, and sump tank.

The surface area of grow media and biological filter media is measured in a sq' per cu' ratio. For each cubic foot of media, imagine the media unzipped and flattened, and then measuring the square footage of the media.

½" Pea Gravel	1" Rock	1" Plastic Biofilter Media	2" Plastic Biofilter Media
85sq' per cu'	21sq' per cu'	85sq' per cu'	48sq' per cu'

Once you've calculated your fish tank volume and biological filter surface area, you should be able to calculate how many pounds of fish your system can support. There are other factors that will influence how well your fish adapt to the system, like dissolved oxygen and nitrite levels, but these can be adjusted after your system is running.

The pH range for each fish should be compared with the pH range of the plants you wish to grow. While most fish can tolerate high pH levels, plants prefer a pH from 6.5-6.8, although many can tolerate neutral pH values.

Fish	pH Range	Temp. Range	Stocking Density	Marketability	Ideal Plant Type
Tilapia	6.8-8.1	74°-88°	Mid/Low	Mid/Low	Warm Season
Trout	6.6-7.8	53°-67°	Mid/Low	Mid/High	Very Cool Season
Koi/G.F.	6.4-8.1	66°-78°	Mid	N/A	Cool Season
Perch	6.6-8.5	67°-78°	Mid	Low	Cool Season
Bluegill	6.9-8.2	68°-82°	High	Very Low	All
Catfish	6.8-8.1	73°-88°	Mid/High	Very Low	Warm Season

Tilapia

- Harvest weight: 16oz-20oz
- Time to harvest: 8-16 months
- Feed: aquatic plants, algae, plant-based manufactured tilapia feed

Tilapia are the easiest, most popular fish for aquaponic systems. They tolerate a wide range of temperatures, stocking densities, and feed rates, while growing to a harvestable rate in less than 18 months.

Tilapia are a warm-water fish, and although they can tolerate cooler temperatures, they prefer a water temperature near 80° throughout the year. This makes them the perfect companion for fruiting vegetables, and a good companion for leafy greens. However, their preference for warm water makes them unable to work well with broccoli and cauliflower.

The biggest drawback to using tilapia is that it can be illegal in some areas to buy and farm. Check with your local extension agent for information on necessary permits for growing tilapia, and make sure you *never* release your tilapia into the wild. It is an invasive fish, and it can destroy habitats very quickly.

Rainbow Trout

- Harvest weight: 16oz-20oz
- Time to harvest: 9-13 months
- Feed: aquatic insects, small fish, manufactured trout feed

Trout are an easy, fast-growing species that are a perfect companion for cool-season crops. Trout must maintain a cool water temperature or else they become stressed, making them susceptible to disease and throwing off your system.

It is much easier to heat water than it is to cool it, which is why trout is generally only used in mild, cooler climates. Trout perform best in a constant-flow system that is over 250 gallons. They are not suited for smaller systems, and they become stressed very quickly in still water.

Trout are the most marketable fish that can be grown in an aquaponic system, so they work very well for growers who want to make a profit from a few focused leafy-green crops, and a modest fish harvest.

The biggest drawback to trout is the temperature and size requirements, but this does make them perfect for large-scale leafy green production in a somewhat controlled climate.

Goldfish/Koi

- Harvest weight: N/A
- Time to harvest: N/A
- Feed: aquatic insects, algae, aquatic plants, manufactured food

Goldfish and koi are more versatile fish as far as the plants they can support, but the obvious disadvantage is that you can't eat them. This makes them perfect for growers who don't eat meat, or have no interest in harvesting fish from the tank.

Another advantage is that goldfish live 5-10 years, and koi can live up to 30 years in a healthy environment. This means that once a system is stocked and ready to plant, you won't need to spend money restocking fish.

One interesting phenomenon of goldfish and koi is that they excrete a chemical into the water that will limit their growth. This is why goldfish stay small in aquariums, when they have the capacity to grow over a foot long in the wild. When water is being circulated through the system, but only a fraction of it is held in the fish tank, the fish may think they have more water to use as a living space than they actually have access to, which can result in oversized fish that become crowded.

Yellow Perch

- Harvest weight: up to 1/2 lb.
- Time to harvest: 1 year
- Feed: aquatic insects, small fish, manufactured food

Perch are a great aquaponic species if you aren't planning on making money on your fish harvest. They tolerate lower pH values, which allow you to cater to the plant's needs more easily. They also tolerate a range of temperatures that makes them a good pair with many plants, and they do well with modest stocking densities.

The biggest drawback for yellow perch is the small harvest size. Perch are not a good choice for growers who want to make a profit from harvesting both sides of their system.

Bluegill

- Harvest weight: 3/4-1 ¼ lb.
- Time to harvest: 2-3 years
- Feed: insects, manufactured food

Bluegill are a popular aquaponic choice in the northern part of the United States, because they have an extremely high stocking density, and they pair well with every vegetable that can be grown in a system.

The biggest consideration with bluegill is the pH, which needs to be at least 6.9 to keep bluegill healthy. They can tolerate a wide range of many other factors, including temperature, but it's important to keep the pH as close to 7 as possible to prevent stress.

The biggest drawback for bluegill is that it takes three years to reach a harvestable size. This makes them a good fish if your focus is plant production, because you won't have to keep purchasing fish for your system, but it limits your profits to vegetables.

Channel Catfish

- Harvest w arvest: 18 months
- Feed: insects, small fish, algae, aquatic plants, manufactured food

Catfish are suitable for aquaponic systems, although it's difficult for them to thrive. Catfish are bottom feeders, which makes tank life a difficult transition.

Catfish are especially susceptible to a disease called *columnaris*, which causes lesions on the gills and fins, and will eventually cause death. This disease can quickly kill an entire tank of catfish, and it can be difficult to detect since it usually hides under the gills.

Water quality is the most important factor for catfish culture. Organic matter in the water (dead plant roots, solid waste, etc.) can feed the bacteria that enable the disease to spread. It's important to maintain bacteria on the surface area of the system to help with filtration, but it's also important to keep your system clean from organic debris to keep the ecosystem in check.

Fish Culture

Once you've decided on the right fish for your system, it's time to stock your tank.

josefkubes/Shutterstock.com

Fry

You will want to purchase your fish as fry from a reputable fish farm. This is the stage just after the fish have absorbed the yolk sac and are able to feed themselves. The amount you feed your fish will be determined by how much they weigh and how old they are, with baby fish eating the most by weight.

Fish that have just begun to feed themselves can eat between 20% and 30% of their body weight in food each day. However, it's best to ask the fish farm what kind of feed and how much they were feeding before shipping. They can give you a good guideline for feed requirements throughout the life of the fish.

The fry stage for fish lasts from a few weeks to a few months.

Fingerling

Once the fish have scales and working fins, they are considered fingerlings. As the name suggests, this generally means the fish are the length of a finger.

This stage has the highest mortality rate, so it's important to keep an eye on your tank and make sure you maintain the right number of fish to support your system. Fingerlings will eat less than fry, but much more than adults. They will also transition into different foods, and it's important to purchase the right food for each stage of life. It's tempting to keep using fry food until you've used up a bag, but it will do more harm than good.

Juvenile

When your fish have grown into a recognizable member of their species, they are considered to be juveniles. Fish in this stage are not able to reproduce, but they are able to be clearly identified by their physical appearance.

Many fish are harvested in the juvenile stage before they reach a mature, breeding age. If your goal is to harvest and sell your fish, research your local markets to see what size they prefer for filets.

If you want to breed your own fish for future use, you will need separate breeding and hatching tanks that can heat or cool water temperatures, reduce or increase water flow, and reduce or increase light to create the appropriate reproduction requirements. Breeding is beyond the scope of this book, and most growers prefer to restock their tanks with fry after each harvest.

Feeding

Fry can eat up to 30% of their weight in feed each day, but as the fish mature, they require between 1.5% and 2% of their weight in food each day. Only feed the fish what they will eat in ten minutes, and if you notice leftover food, try cutting back until there is no more than 5% of the feed leftover after 10 minutes.

If the water temperature or pH fluctuate too much, or become too high or low for the fish, they will stop eating and this can cause a system crash. Consistent testing and logging will help you determine the best maintenance schedule for efficient feeding.

Cycling

Before fish and plants can grow in your system, nitrifying and mineralizing bacteria need to establish a healthy colony. These bacteria will transform fish waste into plant nutrients, but they need time to find your system and set up camp.

There are two methods of cycling:

- Fish cycling
- Fishless cycling

Obviously, the difference between the two is whether or not fish are involved. Fish cycling is the more natural method of building up bacteria, but it takes longer and can be more stressful for your fish. Fishless cycling is shorter, but it involves adding ammonia manually, which some growers dislike.

The purpose of cycling is to add ammonia into the system to attract nitrifying bacteria. This will build up the biological filter that cleans the water, which will keep ammonia from reaching toxic levels for the fish. Once this process is complete, your system will be able to transform ammonia into nitrate, and it will be ready for a full fish tank and grow beds.

Fish Cycling

Fish cycling is the more natural, traditional method of cycling a new aquaponic system. This process takes up to 6 weeks, and will require daily water tests to check ammonia levels.

The key to fish cycling is to build up your bacteria slowly by only adding a few fish at a time. Start with a few fish, preferably goldfish, and feed them small amounts of food. Goldfish handle ammonia and pH fluctuations better than other aquaponic fish, and they are easy to replace if a few die off.

As the fish produce waste, nitrifying bacteria will be attracted to the system. The bacteria will start transforming ammonia into nitrates, which are harmless to fish. However, to avoid high nitrate levels, which can cause an algae bloom, you can put a few plants into your grow beds.

You should begin testing your water before you add any fish. Get a baseline pH, temperature, and ammonia reading, and then add in a few fish. They will begin to produce ammonia as soon as they are in the water, so it's important to have your pumps and filters working to avoid ammonia toxicity.

Many freshwater tests measure total ammonia, which is the total ammonia *and* nitrate in the system. It's almost impossible to distinguish between toxic ammonia and beneficial nitrate on a test, but an increase likely signals a rise in ammonia.

The only way to keep ammonia in check is to monitor pH and temperature. Nitrifying bacteria operate better in a pH range of 6.8-7, and in cooler temperatures. Cover your fish tank and grow beds to prevent the water from getting too warm, and keep close tabs on temperature fluctuations. As long as the pH remains right below neutral, the bacteria should have the right environment to filter the water.

If your test shows a spike in ammonia, you may have to replace a large amount of water. Ammonia can quickly build up and kill your fish, so if you notice the ammonia levels climbing above 5ppm, prepare 1/3 of the water volume of your system by adjusting the pH and temperature to the proper levels. The pH should be close to 7, and within .3 of the system water, and the temperature should be within 3° of the system water to prevent shocking the fish. Drain off 1/3 of the system water, and add the new water. Repeat a water test to make sure this lowered the ammonia below 5ppm.

Ammonia and nitrate are difficult to distinguish on a water test, but once your *nitrite* levels are consistently measuring near 0.5ppm, you have established both types of nitrifying bacteria that are necessary for nitrification. This will take at least a few weeks, but will more likely take a month or two.

Once bacteria have colonized your system, you can gradually introduce more fish and plants. Add half of your fish and plants, and keep testing your water daily. If the nitrite levels remain steady, your system has been successfully cycled, and you can add the rest of the fish and plants, and resume a normal feeding ratio.

Fishless Cycling

This cycling process is similar to fish cycling, but it can tolerate fluctuations because there are no fish in the system. It also establishes nitrifying bacteria faster, and it is easier to amend the water to reach the right pH and ammonia levels. Fishless cycling can prepare your system for fish in 2-3 weeks.

Fishless cycling requires adding pure ammonia in low doses to encourage nitrifying bacteria. You can use either pure, 100% liquid ammonia from a hardware store, or crystalized ammonia that is formulated for aquaponic systems.

Put a few plants into the system, and start adding ammonia in very low doses. Each day, increase the amount of ammonia you add until you reach 5ppm on your water test. Keep a log of the pH, water temperature, and amount of ammonia you added to maintain 5ppm.

Once you have consistent readings of 5ppm ammonia, begin testing for nitrites. Once nitrites climb to 0.5ppm, cut the amount of ammonia you are using by half. Nitrate levels should climb over 5ppm, while nitrite levels taper off. When the nitrite levels reach 0, your system has been successfully cycled. You can now add plants and fish, but continue to test the water, pH, and temperature to keep ammonia levels in check.

Once your system has been successfully cycled, you must continue to monitor the water quality to ensure the health of your plants and fish. Fluctuations due to pH, temperature, and feeding ratios can throw off the balance of your entire system and cause a system crash.

Feeding requirements change throughout the life of the fish, and this will affect the amount and quality of the waste that the fish produce. It's important to keep testing ammonia, nitrate, and nitrite levels to make sure you are feeding the right amount each day.

We will cover testing and adjusting these nutrients more in the next chapter.

Nitrification, Mineralization, & Oxygenation

While aquaponics is generally described as using fish waste to feed plants, this isn't technically true. Organic fertilizers, like animal waste, actually provide food for bacteria, which then provide nutrition for plants.

This is why the bacterial health of an aquaponic system is so crucial. Without a healthy population of the right bacteria, the fish waste would pass right by the plant roots and back into the fish tank, killing the fish and plants within a matter of days.

The three driving processes behind a healthy system are nitrification, mineralization, and oxygenation.

Nitrification refers to transforming ammonia into nitrites, and then into nitrates, which is a plant-soluble form of nitrogen.

Mineralization refers to the process of transforming the rest of the fish waste into all the other nutrients that plants need to grow.

Oxygenation refers to adding and maintaining dissolved oxygen levels in the water so that the fish can breathe, and so the bacteria are able to continue transforming waste into nutrients.

All three of these processes are influenced by water temperature, air temperature, pH, mechanical filtration, biological filtration, water circulation, fish feed, fish species, plant species, light, and water quality.

The majority of the labor involved with maintaining an aquaponic system is testing, logging, and adjusting these factors. A large part of aquaponics is chemistry, and there is no such thing as a successful aquaponic system without a basic understanding of how plants absorb nutrients.

Nitrification

Nitrification is the most important chemical process in an aquaponic system.

Fish excrete ammonia from their gills, and this ammonia can quickly build up and become toxic if it's not removed from the water. Ammonia (NH3) is a gas, and is constructed with one nitrogen atom and three hydrogen atoms.

Nitrosomonas is the most common bacteria associated with transforming ammonia into nitrite. These bacteria oxidize the ammonia, which forms the equally-toxic, but necessary, chemical compound N02-.

The equation for this process looks like this:

NH3 (ammonia) + 02 (oxygen) = NO2 (nitrogen dioxide) + 3h+ (hydrogen ions) + 2e- (electrons)

In layman's terms, bacteria mix ammonia and oxygen together to form nitrite. A byproduct of this process is hydrogen ions, which is what is measured during a pH test. So, the first step of nitrification will provide nitrite, *and* lower the pH of the water.

Nitrobacter is the most common bacteria associated with transforming nitrite into nitrate. These bacteria oxidize the nitrites, which form the plant-soluble, non-toxic chemical compound NO_3^-.

The equation for this process looks like this:

NO_2^- (nitrogen dioxide) + H_2O (water) = NO_3 (nitrate) + $2H^+$ (hydronium ions) + $2e^-$ (electrons)

This process produces a form of nitrogen, NO_3, which plants can absorb. Hydronium ions are also produced, which will lower the pH of the water.

Both ammonia and nitrites are toxic to fish, so it's important for the nitrification process to clean the water thoroughly as it circulates through the filters and grow beds. The most important factor in this process is BSA, or biological surface area.

Biological Surface Area

Biological surface area (BSA) is any surface area within your system, although the most important are your grow beds and biological filters. The more surface area, the more bacteria can colonize your system. As bacteria grow and reproduce, they become more effective at nitrifying the ammonia.

This is why media-filled beds are able to support plants with heavy nitrogen needs. The grow media provides a lot of surface area for bacteria, which transforms large amounts of waste into nitrogen. It also helps support a higher stocking density in your fish tank, because it can filter out waste at a higher rate than a DWC system.

This is also why many media-bed growers prefer clay pebbles over other media options. Porous grow media adds even more surface area for bacteria, which helps filter the water better, and feeds plants the maximum amount of nitrogen.

However, a biological filter can achieve the same results as a media bed, which is why you *must* add one into a DWC system. These filters add a large amount of surface area, just like a media bed, where bacteria can colonize and nitrify ammonia.

BSA is calculated by finding the square footage per cubic foot. Porous grow media, like clay pebbles, have a large amount of surface area, but they take up very little space. Once you choose your grow media or biofilter media, calculate the volume it will occupy, and research the square footage per cubic foot for your media

Media	½" Gravel	1" Rock	1" Plastic Bio Balls	2" Plastic Bio Balls
Sq' per Cu'	85sq'	21sq'	85sq'	48sq'

For example, if you have a grow bed that is 4' x 8' x 14", and you want to fill it 12" deep, then you will have 32 cubic feet of grow bed space. If you use 1" rock as your media, you can calculate your BSA by multiplying the square footage area of 1" rock (21sq') by the amount of cubic feet in your grow bed (32').

The math will look something like this:

4' x 8' x 1' = 32cu'

21 x 32 = 672sq' of surface area in 32cu' of grow bed space.

With a low stocking density of 1lb of fish per 10 gallons of tank water, you need at least 25sq' of BSA per pound of fish.

So, if you have 672sq' of BSA in your grow media (not including the surface area of your grow bed) then you could support at least 26 lbs of fish with your grow bed. If you want a higher stocking density, you may need as much as 50sq' of BSA per pound of fish.

pH

The pH values of your system have a substantial effect on the nitrification process. Nitrification will result in a lower pH value, but if a pH value is too low, nitrification will slow down or halt. Consequently, the pH may begin to rise, but not before your plants and fish suffer.

If pH adjustments are made gradually, the bacteria can usually acclimate and nitrification will proceed as usual. However, large doses of pH modifiers can kill off the bacteria that enable nitrification, which can cause a system crash.

A pH between 6.2 and 6.8 seems to be ideal for nitrifying bacteria, although they will still function at neutral. If you need to adjust the pH of your system, do so gradually and before the pH dips below 6, in order to preserve the health of your bacteria.

Temperature

Temperature has an effect on nitrifying bacteria, although the margin for error is much wider than other factors. Nitrifying bacteria operate best between 85° and 95°, although they are plenty active down to 59° where there's a steep decline in efficiency.

This is good news for aquaponics growers, because most systems will operate between 60° and 80°. Plants that need more nitrogen are generally warm-season plants, which also happen to be closer to the sweet spot of nitrification. Leafy greens need more nitrogen than other nutrients, but are much less demanding overall, and can tolerate lower nitrification rates and lower temperatures.

Testing

The only way to gauge the health of your system (before a system failure) is with consistent water tests. Any freshwater test that shows nitrate, nitrite, and ammonia will help you determine how well your system is converting ammonia into nitrogen.

In general, you should aim for the following numbers:

- Total Ammonia Nitrogen: <1ppm
- Nitrite: <1ppm
- Nitrate: 5-150ppm
- Dissolved Oxygen: 5ppm

Ammonia and nitrite are extremely toxic for fish, so it's important to take corrective action quickly if you notice a rise in either value. Nitrates are harmless up to 160ppm, but large numbers at the end of your system (before reentry into the fish tank) suggests your system can feed more plants or heavier nitrogen users.

Extremely low values suggest the opposite; your system is maxed out and may be suffering from nitrogen deficiency.

Nitrogen Deficiency

Regular testing should alert you to nitrogen deficiencies before your plants, but it's important to recognize the signs.

The most obvious sign of nitrogen deficiency is yellow leaves. Nitrogen is responsible for green, fleshy growth, so yellow, stunted plants are a classic symptom of nitrogen deficiency. However, it can also be a sign of other problems, like lack of appropriate lighting, or other nutrient deficiencies and toxicities.

Lertwit Sasipreyajun/Shutterstock.com

The best way to diagnose nitrogen deficiencies is by testing the water. If the nitrates are relatively high (above 40ppm), check the other nutrients and the quality of light.

Denitrification

Denitrification occurs when oxygen levels are low, and anaerobic bacteria break down nitrates into N2O (nitrous oxide) and N2 (nitrogen gas). This removes plant-soluble nitrogen from the water, and releases hydroxide.

The bacteria that facilitate this process are called *facultative heterotrophic bacteria.* A facultative organism is one that uses oxygen for energy, but *can* use other sources of energy when there is no other choice.

Heterotrophic bacteria gain organic compounds by consuming other living organisms. All organic material contains carbon, so these bacteria will grow in piles of solids within your system, and anywhere dead leaves or roots may accumulate.

So, facultative heterotrophic bacteria need carbon to survive, and prefer oxygen for metabolism, but *if given no other choice,* they will metabolize nitrogen.

In layman's terms, this means that this bacteria like oxygen in order to eat piles of waste and dead plant material. However, if dissolved oxygen is not available, they will break down NO3 (nitrate) to consume the nitrogen. Therefore, denitrification only happens in pockets of your system with low oxygen levels and solid waste or plant material.

This will most likely occur in the corners of your grow bed, in the sludge layer of your grow media, and in your filters.

While denitrification sounds harmful, it can be quite useful in moderation. One byproduct of this chemical process is hydroxide, which has the opposite effect of hydronium. Both are hydrogen ions, but hydronium acidifies the water, while hydroxide alkalizes the water.

So, in a system where nitrification produces an overabundance of nitrates, and lowers the pH, denitrification can remove the excess nitrates, and balance the pH by raising it. While nitrates are harmless to fish, if the plants cannot remove all the nitrates within a system, algae may begin to grow out of control within your system.

The key to managing nitrification and denitrification is to resist the urge to clean the parts of your system that have a healthy buildup of bacteria, and to keep an eye on water flow and solids buildup to prevent too many pockets of anaerobic bacteria. Your system should circulate the water completely once per hour, and proper aeration will ensure there is plenty of oxygen for bacteria.

Mineralization

Nitrification is the process that turns liquid waste into nitrogen. Mineralization is the process that turns solid waste into the eleven other nutrients that plants need to grow:

- Phosphorus
- Potassium
- Calcium
- Magnesium
- Sulfur
- Copper
- Zinc
- Iron
- Manganese
- Molybdenum
- Boron

Fish feces already contain these chemical elements, but they are unable to be absorbed by the plants. Bacteria must break down the waste and release the compounds so that the plants are able to use them.

Mineralization can occur in aerobic or anaerobic conditions, although aerobic mineralization is much better for your system. Anaerobic mineralization can have harmful byproducts that disrupt the ecosystem in your grow beds and fish tanks.

As bacteria breaks down solid waste, they also produce ammonia. This can help fuel nitrification if there are strong amounts of nitrifying bacteria. However, if the system is low on dissolved oxygen, ammonia can buildup and harm your fish.

Mineralization will also break down excess fish food, and release those compounds as plant-soluble nutrients. However, fish waste is a much better source of nutrition, so it's important to try to meet their needs as accurately as possible.

Mineralization Tanks

The bacteria that break down solid waste need surface area to colonize. This is the purpose of the mineralization tanks. They are large tanks filled with a media that provides a large surface area, and as solid waste flows into the tank, it is trapped by the media and begins to decompose.

The difference between biological surface area for nitrification, and biological surface area for mineralization, is that nitrification works on the ammonia in the water, while mineralization works on settled solids. The surface area on the sides of a grow bed does not help with mineralization, because there's no buildup of solid waste.

Macro and Micro nutrients

Frequent water testing will help to keep your system balanced. Each nutrient is necessary for certain plant functions, and each one can cause problems if it is outside its optimal range.

Potassium

This nutrient is responsible for communication between plant cells, and it regulates many chemical processes. It's also the most common deficiency in an aquaponic system, since fish feed is not manufactured to keep up with the needs of plants.

Mineralization will only break down the elements that are already present. If fish feed is lacking in certain nutrients, no amount of mineralization can make up for them. Therefore, if you are using an aquaculture feed instead of an aquaponic feed, you will end up with potassium deficiencies.

There are a few simple ways to solve this, but the most common is potassium hydroxide. This will add potassium into the system, but hydroxide will also raise the pH, so it's important to keep an eye on both the nutrient levels and the pH levels before adding any chemical to your system.

Phosphorus

Phosphorus is responsible for healthy root growth, which is critical for aquaponic plants. The roots are constantly submerged, so an unhealthy root system will quickly rot in this environment.

Leafy greens have smaller root systems, so they don't need as much phosphorus. Fruiting crops have a more complex root system, so they need more phosphorus. Fish can handle large amounts of phosphorus in the water, although too much may cause an algae bloom.

Phosphorous deficiencies are difficult to diagnose until they are severe. Dark green, red, or purple growth near the base of the plant is one unique sign of a deficiency. Other symptoms, like stunted growth, can mimic other problems. Correct a phosphorus deficiency with granulated phosphate, and apply it directly to the grow beds. Avoid supplementing plants that do not produce fruit.

Calcium

This is a difficult nutrient to manage, because calcium amendments almost always raise pH values. If your system could use a pH boost, then adding calcium may benefit the plants, but if your water is already alkaline, this may not be possible.

Calcium deficiencies can result in stunted and deformed plants. Calcium gives plants structure and strength, so a deficiency will result in lopsided and weak plant structures.

You can add calcium to your system with agricultural lime, which will also add raise magnesium. Calcium, magnesium, and sulfur are all closely intertwined, and many treatments for deficiencies will affect all three nutrients.

Lime will raise the pH, which is fine if your pH is low. However, if you don't want to risk a pH fluctuation, you can apply calcium chloride with a foliar spray.

Magnesium

Magnesium builds chlorophyll, which is the driving force behind photosynthesis. If there is not enough magnesium in the system, photosynthesis will suffer, and plants will not have enough energy to maintain growth.

Magnesium deficiencies result in green veins with yellow leaf tissue. Older growth will die off as the plant pulls magnesium from older growth to sustain new growth.

Agricultural lime will add magnesium as well as calcium, while simultaneously raising the pH of the water. Calcium toxicities are rare, so adding lime for a magnesium boost should not overload your system with calcium.

You can also use Epsom salt as a magnesium amendment, but you must be careful that you don't add too much. Epsom salt is not salt, so it won't kill plants like salt will. However, too much can cause many issues. Use an average of 1 tablespoon per 1,000 gallons to correct magnesium or sulfur deficiencies.

Sulfur

Calcium, magnesium, and sulfur are difficult to separate. They all serve different functions, but amending one will affect all three.

Sulfur deficiencies are rare. Sulfates tend to build up in an aquaponic system; so many times there is an abundance of available sulfur. This nutrient is responsible for healthy, green growth, and a deficiency results in yellow, lanky new stems and leaves. This makes it easy to confuse with other nutrient deficiencies, like phosphorus or nitrogen.

In general, yellow growth is almost never the result of a sulfur deficiency. If you have treated for nitrogen, phosphorus, magnesium, and iron deficiencies, but still have yellow stems, you may be low on sulfur.

Iron

Iron is another important component of photosynthesis. It is also one of the most common deficiencies in aquaponics, aside from potassium and calcium. While technically a micronutrient, it is a common problem in aquaponic systems, so it is important for diagnosing stressed plants.

Iron deficiencies result in chlorosis, or yellow leaves. A simple nutrient test should help clarify which nutrient is causing chlorosis, because this is a common symptom of many deficiencies.

Once you have confirmed an iron deficiency, the best remedy is chelated iron, as it is readily available to plants.

Micronutrients

There are other micronutrients that plant a key role in plant development. However, they are rarely deficient or toxic unless the pH of the water is too low or too high.

If your plants are stressed, and other amendments have not helped, it may be time to test and amend trace minerals. However, most problems are solved by adjusting the pH, one of the macronutrients, lighting, or temperature.

Oxygenation

Dissolved oxygen is essential for every process in your aquaponic system. While low oxygen can cause a host of problems, and eventually a system crash, it is incredibly easy to remedy; just add aeration.

It is easy to add dissolved oxygen into a system with an aerator or air stones. Aerators are simple to make with a capped PVC pipe with holes drilled in the side. Air stones are easier to add to grow beds, and they can add quite a bit of dissolved oxygen into your system.

Low oxygen levels can result in anaerobic bacteria, which will begin decomposing waste in ways that are harmful to plants and fish. While healthy nitrifying and mineralizing bacteria release plant-soluble nutrients, anaerobic bacteria release toxic substances that can harm or kill your plants and fish.

One common symptom of low oxygen is the tops of your plants wilting. Wilt in aquaponic plants signals unhealthy roots, which will begin to decay if there is not enough oxygen in the water. Plants need water and oxygen for healthy growth, so a lack of either one will cause wilting.

Another symptom is foul-smelling odors coming from the grow beds, which could signal a buildup of solid waste that has created a pocket of anaerobic bacteria. In a DWC system, you can remove the solid waste or buildup, which will encourage oxygen-rich water to flow into that area again.

In a media-filled bed, it may be more difficult to clean out buildup, which is why redworms are such a popular addition. Worms will break down solids in places where you may not be able to reach, and they will transform waste into plant-soluble nutrients. Worms can survive in water as long as the water has plenty of oxygen. If the worms start dying, you don't have enough aeration.

A third symptom of too little oxygen is fish coming to the surface for air. This needs immediate intervention before your fish suffocate. Add an extra aerator, and consider replumbing the connection between the grow beds and the fish tank to create a waterfall, which adds more oxygen into the water.

A dissolved oxygen meter will measure the amount of oxygen in your water. Cool-water fish require 6.5ppm of dissolved oxygen, while warm-water fish require 5ppm. Warm water will hold less oxygen, so you may need to add more aeration for warm-water fish.

Low oxygen levels are rarely a problem in small hobby operations. As long as stocking densities are not maxed out, and the temperatures are not too high, oxygen should be constant in systems with adequate aeration.

Now that you have chosen a design, fish, and plants, and you understand the science behind aquaponics, you are ready to begin building your system.

Media-Filled Bed

Aquaponic systems are broke up into two main categories: media-filled beds and deep-water culture systems. Both have similar design features, but it's important to understand exactly how and why they differ so you can choose the right system for yourself. The following chapters will explore each system more closely so you can understand the benefits, drawbacks, and design features of each system before you build.

Aquaponic systems are fairly evenly split between what works well for hobby growers and what works well for commercial growers. Commercial systems are not just large-scale hobby operations. They are completely different setups, and they require different inputs and maintenance schedules.

Hobby growers are generally focused on cheaper materials, simpler designs, and a size small enough to be managed by one or two people. In exchange for spending less, they will spend more time maintaining the system, which is a benefit for hobby growers who enjoy the process.

Commercial growers, on the other hand, are focused on the bottom line. They are looking for systems that save them labor time, and those systems are more expensive and complex. Business owners are willing to spend more on certain components if it makes planting, harvesting, and maintenance more efficient. These systems can span acres and involve greenhouses, ventilation fans, heating systems, large filters, multiple fail-safes for pumps, and large labor forces.

While hobby growers use smaller, more labor-intensive systems, that doesn't mean they can't make a profit from their harvest. Many small-scale growers sell produce and fresh fish to neighbors or at local farmers' markets.

There are two main categories of aquaponic systems:

- Media-filled beds
- Deep-water culture (deep-flow, raft, float)

Media-filled beds can either be simple beds, Dutch buckets, or barrelponics. Deep-water channel systems are used on a larger scale, and have been modified into nutrient-film technique systems and vertical designs.

Media-filled beds are used for small to medium-scale operations, and deep-water culture systems are best for medium to large-scale operations.

Media-filled beds provide more stability for fruiting plants, and hold on to more nutrients in the grow beds. This is why most growers who want to use an aquaponic system as a broad-spectrum vegetable garden choose these systems.

Deep-water culture systems lack support for tall plants, and can't hold as much nutrition around the roots of the plants. However, plants grow faster, and can be planted closer together, which makes a deep-channel system perfect for growers who want to focus on one or two crops in larger quantities.

A media-filled bed can circulate water using two different methods; flood and drain, or continuous flow.

In a flood-and-drain system, water is pulled from the fish tank and pushed through a filter every forty-five minutes. Then, it flows from the filter to the grow beds, where it floods the media for fifteen minutes before returning to the fish tank.

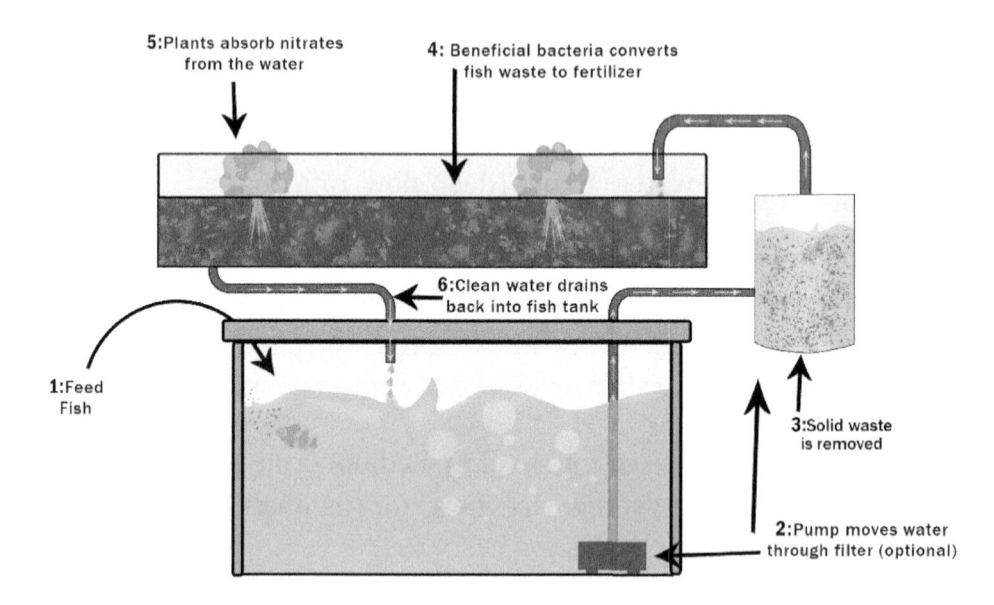

5: Plants absorb nitrates from the water
4: Beneficial bacteria converts fish waste to fertilizer
6: Clean water drains back into fish tank
1: Feed Fish
3: Solid waste is removed
2: Pump moves water through filter (optional)

In a continuous flow system, the water is always flowing from the fish tank, through the filter and grow beds, and then back to the fish tank. This is easier on the fish because the water level in the tank remains constant, but it is more difficult to maintain proper aeration.

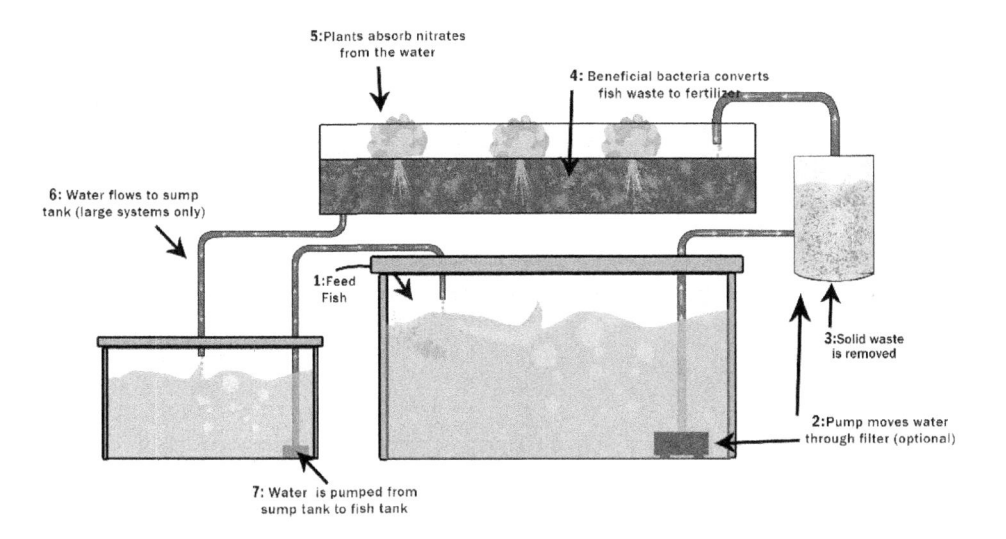

Diagram labels:
- 5: Plants absorb nitrates from the water
- 4: Beneficial bacteria converts fish waste to fertilizer
- 6: Water flows to sump tank (large systems only)
- 1: Feed Fish
- 3: Solid waste is removed
- 2: Pump moves water through filter (optional)
- 7: Water is pumped from sump tank to fish tank

Media-filled beds offer the most diversity for plant selection, and the simplest setup, making them the most popular choice for hobby growers.

Pros:	Cons:
• Simplest system to build	• Extremely heavy; immobile
• Little to no extra filtration needed	• Most expensive to build
• Supports the widest variety of crops	• Labor-intensive
• Provides the best root support	• Must clean media off roots for harvest
• Holds the most nutrients	• Fluctuating water level stresses fish

Pros:	Cons:
• Can add worms for more nutrition	• Slower growth rate than raft systems
• Can be sized very small for class settings	• Not suited for large operations

Growing Media

The media, or *substrate,* that forms the foundation of this system serves four important functions:

- It holds bacteria that turns fish waste into plant nutrients
- It helps oxygenate the water for plant roots and fish
- It serves as a habitat for redworms, which clean the water and provide extra nutrition
- It helps support tall plants

There are a few different options for the substrate you will use in your beds, but they all need to meet four basic requirements:

- Neutral pH
- Inert; meaning it can't break down
- Small enough to allow roots a firm foundation, but large enough to not clog pipes
- Porous enough to allow bacteria to grow on the surface

There are four different growing mediums that meet these requirements:

Pros/Cons	Clay Pebbles	River Rock	Lava Rock	Vermiculite
Lightweight	X		X	X
Smooth	X	X		X
Porous	X		X	X
1" Median Size	X	X		
Estimated Weight per cu'	26lbs	100lbs	44lbs	6lbs
Estimated Cost per cu'	$15-$20	$10-$12	$10-$12	$5-$8
Estimated Cost to fill a 4'x8'x14" bed	$550-$800	$370-$450	$370-450	$200-$310

Of these, clay pebbles and river rock are the most common. Lava rock has sharp edges, which can damage roots easily, and vermiculite is small and can clog pipes and filters.

Clay Pebbles

These pebbles are the easiest media to work with because they are light and smooth.

Clay pebbles are also referred to as LECA (lightweight expanded clay aggregate), and they are basically popped clay. Clay is mined and formed into balls, which are then superheated in a kiln to over 2000° until the clay pops, giving it a light, porous structure.

The most common LECA used for aquaponics is Hydroton. These pebbles come in 50 lb bags, which will fill roughly 2 cubic feet. They are lightweight, so shipping them is much easier than transporting river rock or lava rock.

Clay pebbles are reusable, and provide a smooth surface that does not damage roots. However, they do float for the first few months, and this can cause clogs. You can help prevent this by soaking your pebbles in water for 24 hours before putting them into the grow beds. Make sure the water you use is close to pH neutral and does not contain any harmful chemicals.

Jason Finn/Shutterstock.com

River Rock

Although this is the most expensive option, it is also one of the most popular for grow beds. Costs will vary depending on the supplier, but river rock is generally available at hardware stores and landscape supply companies.

River rock is not porous, but it still has enough surface area for beneficial bacteria to colonize and thrive. It's smooth, which makes planting and harvesting much easier than lava rock, and it doesn't float like Hydroton.

The biggest drawback to river rock is the weight. Systems that use river rock as a substrate will be permanent. One cubic yard of river rock (27 cubic feet) weighs 2,600 lbs. The average 4' x 8' x 14" grow bed will need about 37 cubic feet of media, meaning a bed full of river rock will weigh almost 3,600 lbs.

If you choose to use river rock as a media, rinse it before adding it into your system. River rock is usually coated in a limestone dust, which can raise the pH of the water and harm your plants. Also, the dust and debris that accumulates in piles of river rock at supply companies may cause problems in your system.

Test river rock before you purchase it to see if it will affect the pH of your system. Take a bottle of vinegar and a cup, and fill the cup halfway with rock. Fill the cup with vinegar, and look for fizzing. If it fizzes, the rock has a high pH, and you will want to find another supplier. If the vinegar does not fizz, the rock is pH neutral, and it should be suitable for your system.

The best size for river rock is a 1" median diameter. Too large, and there won't be enough surface area for bacteria to colonize, and the water won't be aerated properly. Too small, and roots may have difficulty finding space to grow.

Lava Rock

Lava rock is the cheapest option for appropriate grow bed media, but it also lacks the most important property of high-quality substrate: smooth edges.

Lava rock is hard on your hands, difficult to maneuver, and cuts through plant roots. The angular shape of lava rock can cause blockages in the beds where algae builds up, and causes pockets of water to remain stagnant.

However, lava rock is also incredibly porous and lightweight, making it a useful addition to a grow bed. Lava rock works best as a layer across the bottom of a bed, where it can serve as a home for bacteria. This will allow you to put a different media on top that's easier on your hands and plant roots. Plus, it helps cut down on the cost of your substrate.

Vermiculite

Vermiculite is manufactured almost exactly like Hydroton; a mined mineral is superheated until it pops, resulting in a lightweight, porous material.

The major problem with vermiculite is that it's small, and can clog pipes or cause blockages. Smaller particle sizes allow roots to form dense mats around them, and this can make harvesting a time-consuming and difficult process.

Vermiculite is best for extremely small aquaponic systems that are used as an educational tool, or as an ingredient in a customized medium.

Please Note: Vermiculite is *not* perlite. While the two have very similar characteristics, perlite contains incredibly small particulates that act like glass shards when they pass through the gills of your fish.

Grow Beds

Grow beds for media-filled bed systems have to meet 3 requirements:

- Support the weight of the growing media, water, and plants
- Composed of a material that can be cut and plumbed
- Provide a smooth, food-safe, pH-neutral surface

The most popular material for grow beds is some type of plastic tub, tote, or bin. These are easy to cut with hole saws, lightweight, and relatively cheap.

Functioning grow beds will be composed of 3 layers:

- Dry Layer (Top)
    - 1"-2" of dry media
    - Prevents algae growth
    - Prevents fungus gnats
- Active Layer (Middle)
    - 8"-9" of biological activity
    - Main filtration area
    - Primary worm habitat

- Sludge Layer (Bottom)
    - 1" or less of solids buildup
    - Harmless if kept in check

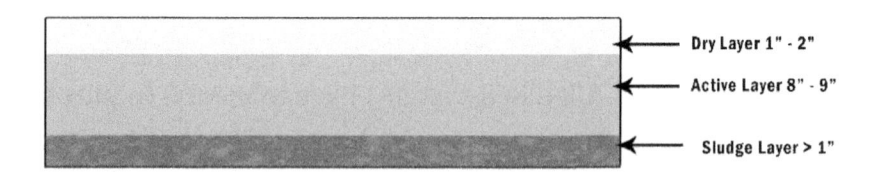

[Diagram showing layers: Dry Layer 1" - 2", Active Layer 8" - 9", Sludge Layer > 1"]

In order to accommodate these layers, a grow bed needs to be at least 12" deep, but it's best to leave a few inches of empty space between the top of the media and the top edge of the grow bed. Ideally, grow beds will be 14" deep.

The most common containers used for grow beds in media-filled systems are:

- IBC totes
- Stock tanks
- Storage barrels/drums
- Household storage totes

Metal containers can leach chemicals into the water, and are unsuitable for any part of an aquaponic system. Wooden frames lined with pond liner are an option, although it works best if the frame is on the ground to support the weight of the media.

As long as a container is at least 12" deep, inert, durable, and workable, it is a candidate for a grow bed. If you have a readily-available supply of containers you want to use as grow beds, find the SPI code to see if they are food safe:

- **1** PET (Polyethylene Terephthalate)
- **2** HDPE (High-Density Polyethylene)
- **4** LDPE (Low-Density Polyethylene)
- **5** PP (Polypropylene)
- ***7** PC (Polycarbonate)
- ***7** uPVC (Unplasticized Polyvinyl Chloride)

*The number "7" on an SPI code means *other plastics,* and includes many plastics that are not food safe.

If you will only have access to your grow bed from one side, limit the width of your bed to 28" or less. If you will be able to access both sides of your grow bed, limit the width to 4' so you can easily reach the center from either side.

Fish and Fish Tanks

The fish in an aquaponic system serve one vital function:

- Digest fish food and excrete ammonia and solid waste

The waste from fish is what provides food for the *bacteria*—not plants—in your system. The bacteria will break down the waste into plant-soluble nutrients, which also cleans the water as it is returned back to the fish tank.

The materials for a fish tank need to meet the same basic requirements as those for grow beds. However, while grow beds should be wide and relatively shallow, fish tanks should be deep with a relatively small diameter. This allows the water in the tank to resist major temperature fluctuations, which stress out the fish.

In a continuous flow system, water is constantly pumped from the tank through the grow beds, and back into the fish tank. This keeps the water at a consistent level, which lowers the stress level on the fish.

However, there are many drawbacks to a continuous flow system with media-filled beds, so most growers opt for a flood-and-drain system with a sump tank. A sump tank will collect water after it drains from the grow beds, and pump it back into the fish tank at an even rate.

Plumbing & Filtration

The plumbing for a media-filled aquaponic system is simpler than other systems, and this makes it easier to maintain. The main plumbing and filtration components required are:

- Siphons to drain the grow beds & fish tank
- Pumps to circulate water
- Aerators to introduce oxygen
- Filters to trap solid waste

The growing medium acts as a bio-filter, which is where bacteria clean the water and transform waste into plant-soluble nutrients.

In a basic setup, water is drained from the fish tank via a U siphon, and passed through a swirl filter to allow solids to settle. Water then flows through and floods the grow beds for 15 minutes, while the bacteria in the grow media clean and filter the water and provide nutrients for the plants.

A bell siphon in the grow bed will drain the water, which may then pass through another solids filter on its way to the sump tank. The sump tank contains a pump that replenishes the water in the fish tank, where the water is aerated and picks up more waste material for the next cycle.

Siphons can either be set on a timer, or built to flood and drain manually. Timers can provide some consistency, but require a backup power source to prevent crop loss in the event of a power outage. Manual siphons are more complex to assemble, but require less energy input and are more reliable.

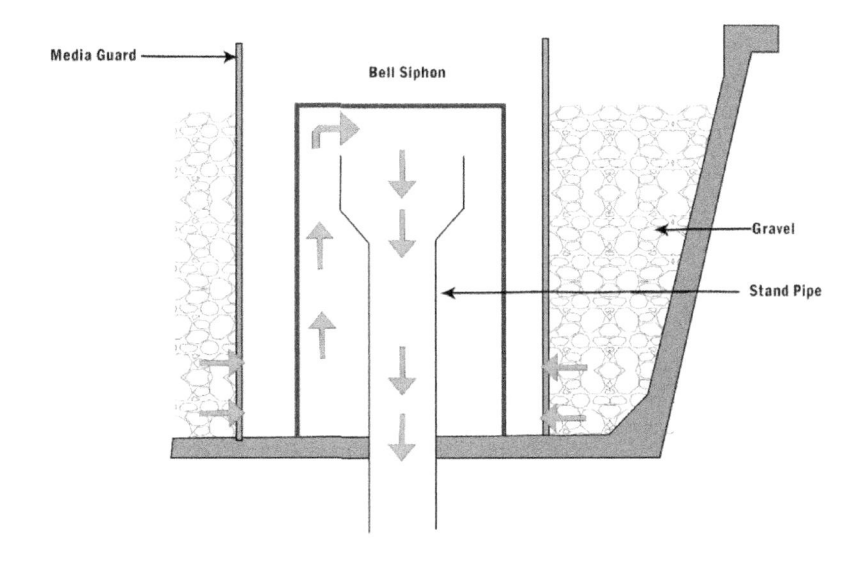

Worms

Perhaps the biggest benefit of a media-filled bed system is the ability to add redworms. One of the most common maintenance issues with this system is the buildup of solids in the growing medium. Redworms feed on dead plant material and fish waste, then excrete castings that are highly-nutritious for vegetables. This helps keep the bottom sludge layer from causing clogs, and also prevents dead zones of deoxygenated water.

Worms must be clean before they are added into an aquaponic system. Manure worms or worms from a compost pile may carry pathogens that are harmful to humans, like E. coli. Purchase worms from a reputable supplier who ships them in peat moss. When you receive them, separate the worms from the moss and rinse them well.

Worms can survive in either flood-and-drain or continuous flow systems as long as the water is well aerated. They absorb oxygen from the water through their skin, and they can climb up through the media to the surface if needed.

Media-filled beds offer the widest crop selection and the simplest design. They work well for beginners who want a smaller system with a forgiving margin of error. However, they are difficult to maintain on a large scale, and the setup cost is higher than a deep-channel system.

If you've mastered the media bed, or you want to focus on higher yield with fewer crops, it's time to move into a deep-channel system.

Building a Media-Filled Bed System

A basic media-filled bed system has the following components:

- Fish Tank
- Aerator
- Water Pump
- Grow Bed
- Grow Media
- Siphons
- Plumbing

You may also decide to include an extra solids filter and an extra BSA filter. Once you've decided on the size of your system, the design is simple to scale up or down.

There are three basic media-filled bed designs:

- 10-gallon fish tank
- Stacked tanks
- IBC totes

Each system is a similar design, but on a larger or smaller scale. A 10-gallon tank design will support a few goldfish and a few heads of lettuce or herbs. Stacked totes or tanks will support 10-20 fish and provide 4' x 2.5' of growing area. IBC totes can support 25-50 fish and multiple 4' x 4' grow beds.

10-Gallon Tank

Pros	Cons
- Easy to use indoors	- Small growing space
- Easy to observe fish	- Does not support harvestable fish
- Easy to set up	- Does not support fruiting vegetables
- Educational	- Not profitable

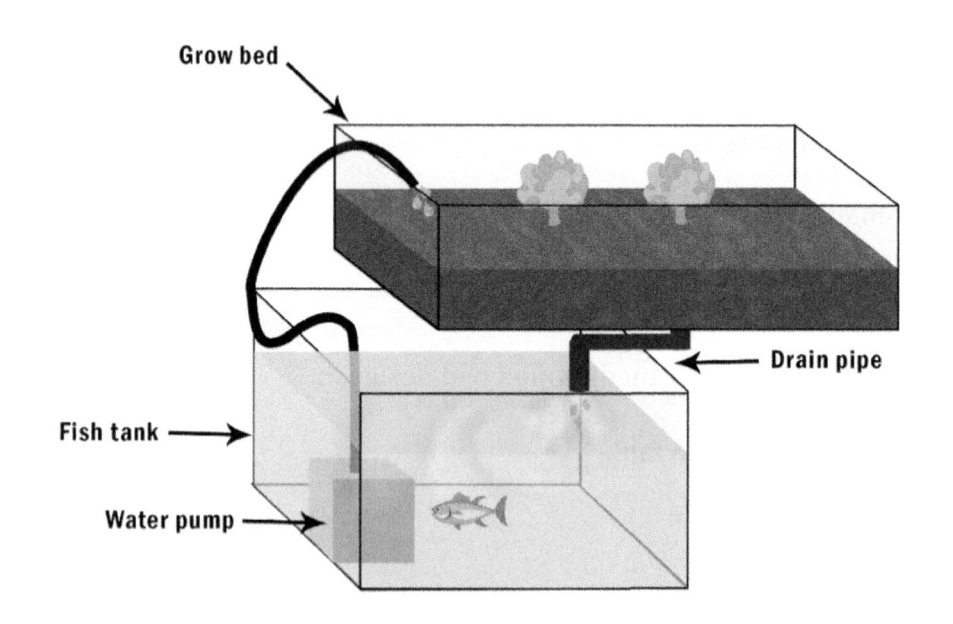

A 10-gallon tank system is best for small, educational purposes. This system is relatively cheap, and will support a few heads of lettuce or a small herb garden.

Materials:

- 10-gallon fish tank **$15**
- 5lbs. Aquarium gravel **$10**
- Small fountain water pump (20"-35" of lift @50 gallons/hour) **$50**
- 3' plastic tubing with the same diameter as your water pump **$3**
- 10-gallon aquarium air pump **$20**
- 2" air stone **$8**
- 3' air pump tubing (must be the same size as air pump outlet & fit air stone) **$2**
- 8" deep plastic bin that sits on top of fish tank **$15**
- Vermiculite, clay pebbles, or river rock **$15**
- Test kit for pH **$25**
- Test kit for ammonia **$15**
- Aquarium thermometer **$5**
- 3-5 goldfish **$20**
- 2' x 1' Grow light **$40**
- Grow media

Total Estimated Cost: $243

Tools:

- Drill
- 3/16" drill bit
- ½" drill bit
- Scissors
- Electrical tape

Directions[1]

Step 1.

Fill a 30-gallon container with water. While your tank is only 10 gallons, it will hold more than this due to the grow bed and plumbing. Prepare 30 gallons so you can completely fill your system when it is finished. Use a pH meter to test your water, and adjust it if necessary to reach a neutral reading. Allow the water to sit 24 hours for chlorine to dissipate.

Step 2.

Rinse aquarium gravel and aquarium thoroughly. Put gravel in the aquarium.

Step 3.

Drill holes spaced 2" apart in the bottom of the grow bed using the 3/16" drill bit.

---

[1] System from Nelson Pade: https://aquaponics.com/aquaponics-information/build-a-mini-aquaponic-system/

Step 4.

Drill one hole through a back corner of the grow bed with the ½" drill bit.

Step 5.

Put the water pump in the fish tank. Connect the tubing to the water pump, and put it through the ½" hole in the grow bed. Place the grow bed on top of the aquarium.

Step 6.

Fill the grow bed half full with grow media. Poke holes every few inches along the water pump tubing. Seal the end of the tubing with electrical tape.

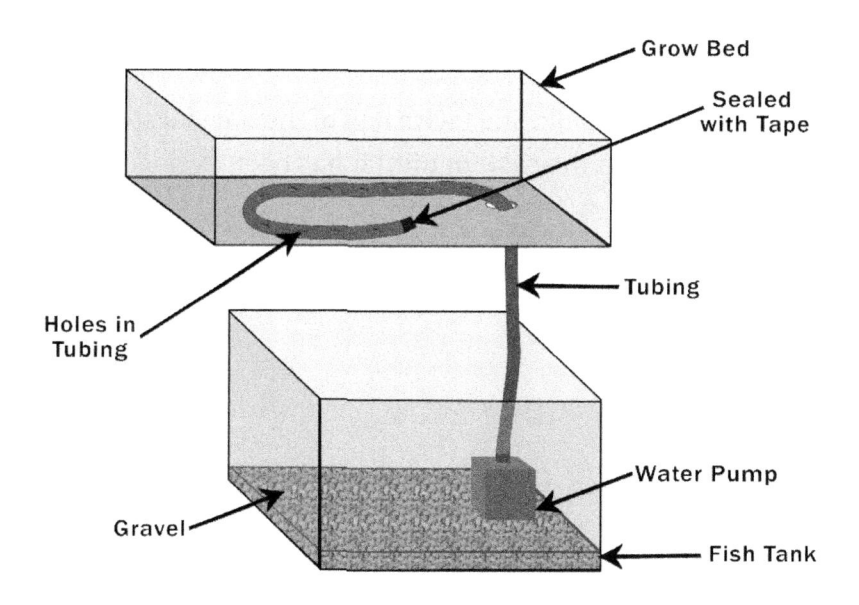

Step 7.

Loop the tubing around inside the grow bed. Fill the rest of the grow bed with media, leaving 1" of empty space below the lip of the grow bed.

Step 8.

Fill the fish tank with the treated water, and turn on the water pump. Water should flow up the tubing, seep out the holes, and trickle back down through the media and into the fish tank.

Step 9.

Connect the air stone to the air pump with the tubing. Put the air stone in the tank, and plug in the pump.

Step 10.

Add goldfish to the fish tank. Start with half of the normal stocking rate, so put 2-3 goldfish into the system until it has been cycled.

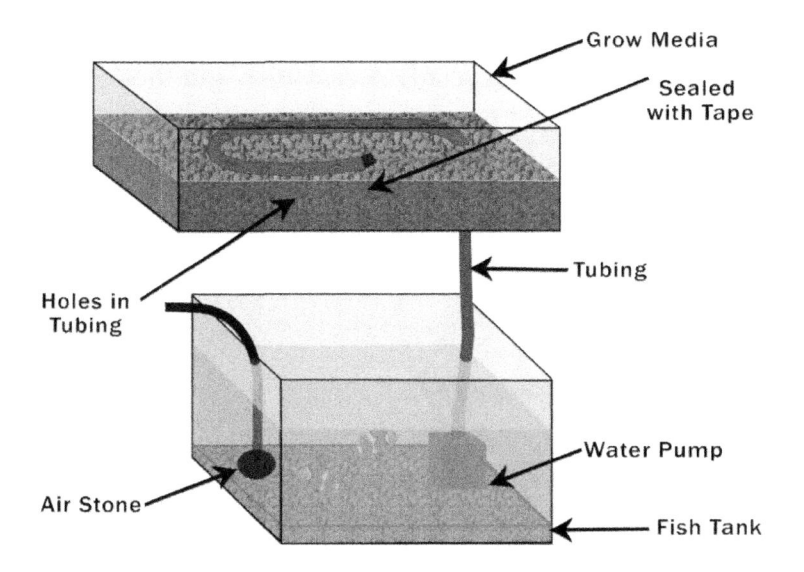

Step 11.

Your system should be ready to support small plants in a few weeks. Once your system has been cycled successfully, add the rest of the fish and plant some seedlings. Continue to monitor the water temperature, pH, and ammonia levels to keep your fish and plants happy.

sharohyip/Shutterstock.com

Stacked Tanks

Pros	Cons
• Indoor/Outdoor use	• Not an attractive setup
• Budget-friendly	• Difficult to expand
• Provides food for 1 person	• Not profitable

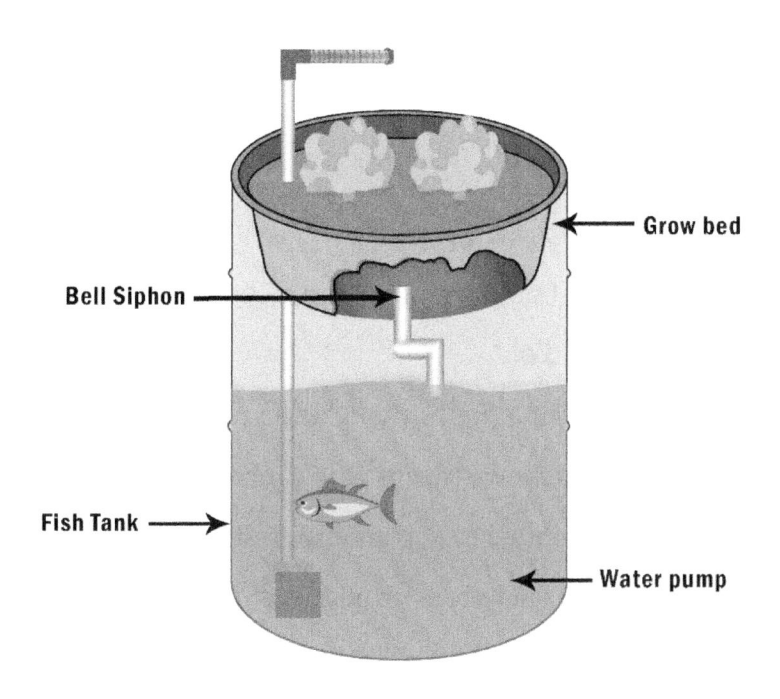

Stacked tanks can range from barrels to IBC totes, and can be scaled up or down easily. They are best for growers who want to supplement their own food supply with plant material. These systems do not support enough fish for consistent harvest.

Make sure all materials meet the standards outlined in the media-filled bed chapter.

Materials:

- 1- 55-gallon plastic barrel **$50**
- 1- 200 gallon/hour water pump **$30**
- 1- ½" male threaded to slip adapter (water pump) **$.50**
- 1- ½" female threaded to slip adapter (water pump) **$.50**
- 1- ½" 90° elbow (water pump) **$.50**
- 1- ½" cap **$.50**
- 3' of ½" PVC pipe **$3**
- 2- #18 O-rings (siphon connection) **$2**
- 2- #14 O-rings **$2**
- 18" of ¾" PVC pipe (bell siphon, drain pipe) **$5**
- 2- ¾" 90° PVC elbows (drain pipe connection) **$.50**
- 1- ¾" male threaded to slip adapter (siphon connection) **$.50**
- 1- ¾" female threaded to slip adapter (siphon connection) **$.50**
- 1- ¾"-1 ½" bell adapter (bell siphon) **$3**
- 8" of 2" PVC pipe (bell dome) **$1**
- 1- 2" PVC cap (bell dome) **$1**
- 10" of 3" PVC pipe (media guard) **$3**

- 1- 3" PVC cap **$2**
- Grow media

Total Estimated Cost: $105.50

Tools:

- 100% silicone
- Caulk gun
- Permanent marker
- Tool capable of cutting holes in PVC and plastic

Directions[2]

Step 1.

Cut the top 12" off the top of the barrel. This section will be your grow bed. Smooth the cut edges with sandpaper, and rinse out the barrel.

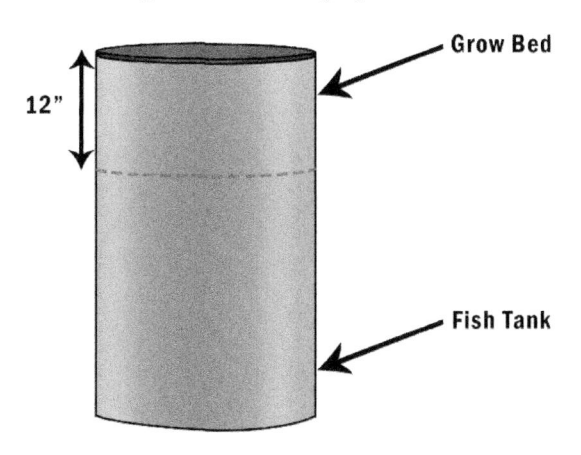

---

[2] System design from: https://www.instructables.com/id/Barrelponics-Getting-Started-With-Aquaponics

Step 2.

Use the ¾" male threaded to slip adapter to trace an intake hole on one side of the bottom of the grow bed. Cut out the hole.

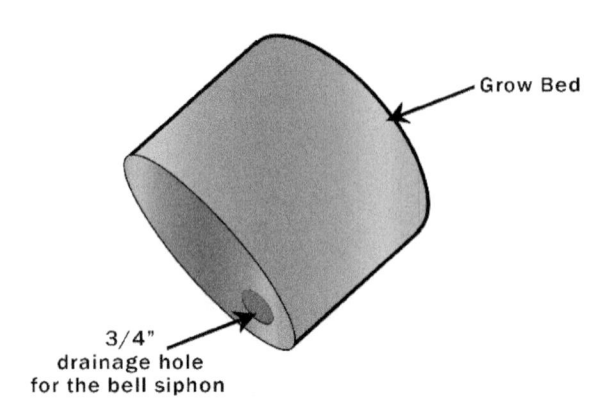

Grow Bed

3/4"
drainage hole
for the bell siphon

Step 3.

Use the ½" male threaded to slip adapter to trace an intake hole on the other side of the grow bed. Cut out the hole.

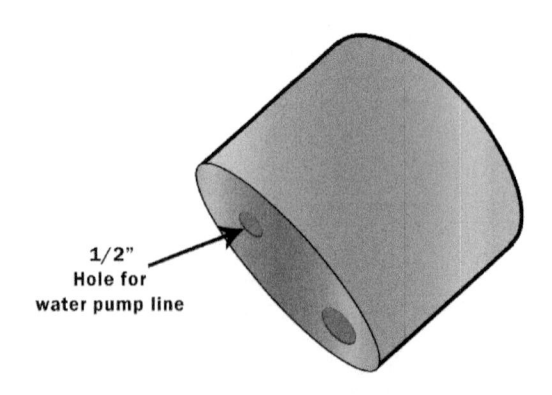

1/2"
Hole for
water pump line

Step 4.

Place the grow bed upside down on top of the barrel. Mark an area for fish access, and cut out a hole. The hole needs to be big enough to use a small net to manage fish. Allow enough room for the grow bed to sit firmly on top of the barrel, but don't cut too low or else you will lower the capacity of your fish tank.

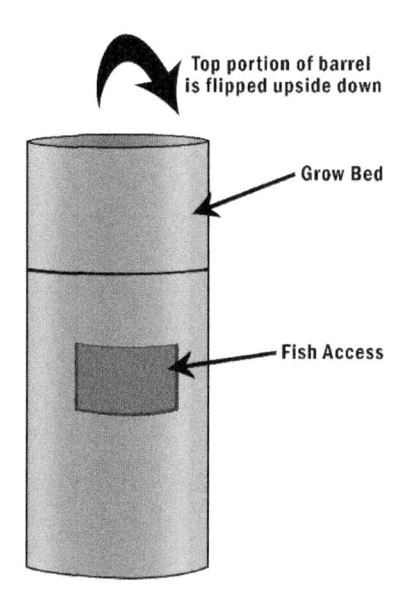

Step 5.

Cut a small hole in back of the barrel near the top for the water pump's power cord.

Step 6.

Drill 8 holes around the bottom of the grow bed through the solid lip of the edge of the barrel. Drill 8 matching holes in the top of the fish tank. When the bell siphon and water pump have been connected, you will thread zip ties through these holes to hold the grow bed onto the fish tank.

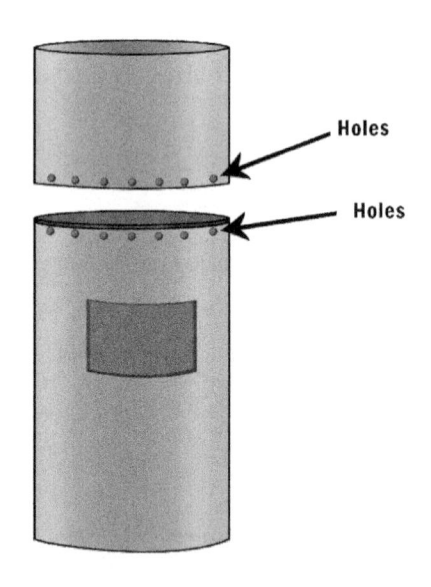

Step 7.

Build the bell siphon

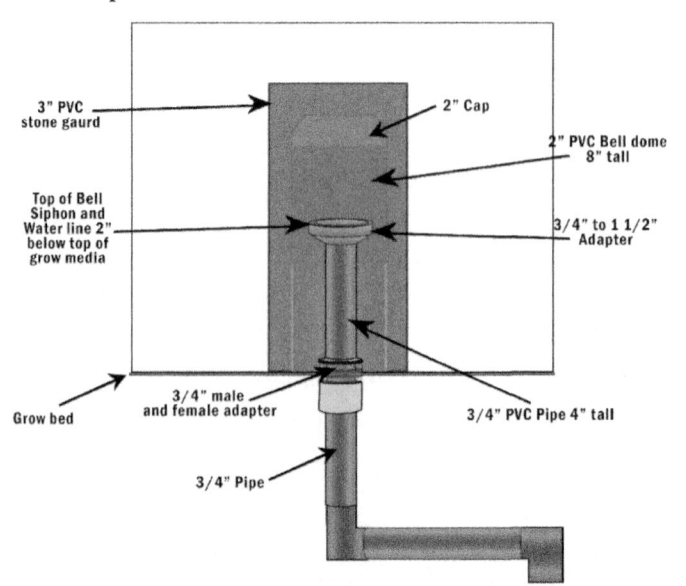

- Put one #18 o-ring over the threads of the ¾" male adapter.
- Push the male adapter up through the hole in the bottom of the grow bed.

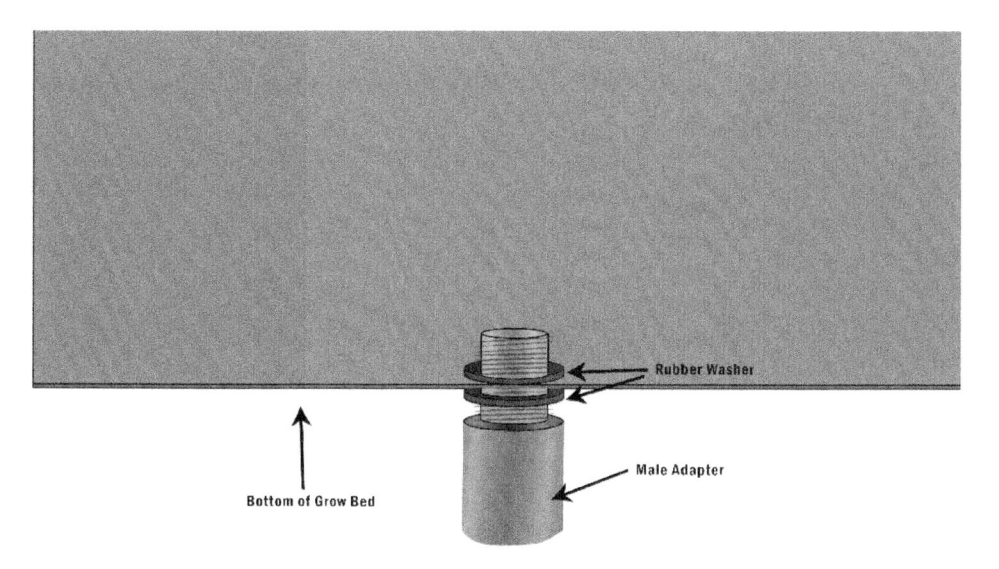

- Put the second #18 o-ring over the threads of the male adapter, and attach the ¾" female adapter. Hand tighten.

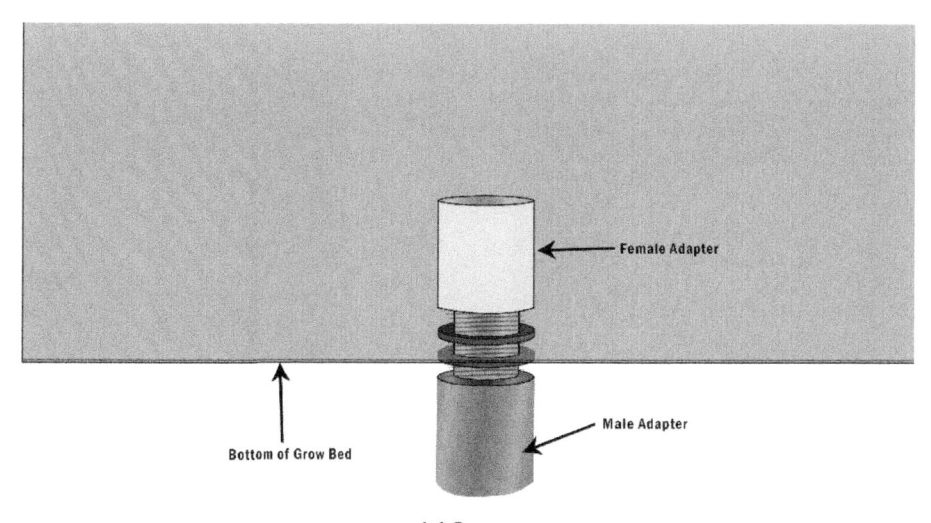

- Cut a 6" piece of ¾" PVC, and place it over the female adapter. (You may need to adjust this depending on your water level)
- Put the ¾"- 1/1/2" adapter on top of the ¾" PVC pipe.
- Use a circular saw or small drill bit to cut notches in the bottom ½" of the 2" PVC pipe. This will allow water through the bottom of the bell.

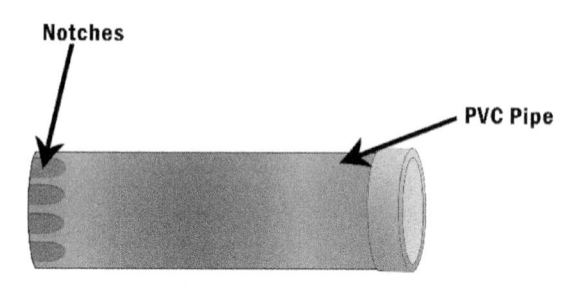

Notches

PVC Pipe

- Place the 8" piece of 2" PVC over the adapter. Put the 2" cap on top.
- Use a circular saw or small drill bit to cut holes or lines in the 3" piece of PVC. This is the gravel guard, which allows water to reach the siphon, but keeps out the grow media.

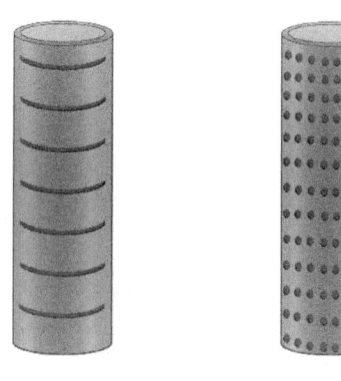

- Place the gravel guard over the 2" PVC pipe.
- Place the 3" cap on the 3" gravel guard.
- Cut a 4" piece of ¾" PVC and attach it to the underside of the male adapter.
- Attach one ¾" 90° elbow at the end of the ¾" PVC pipe.
- Cut an 8" piece of ¾" PVC pipe and attach it to the 90° elbow.
- Attach the other ¾" 90° elbow to the end of the ¾" PVC pipe.

Step 8.

Put one #14 o-ring over the threads of the ½" male adapter. Push the male adapter up through the corresponding hole in the bottom of the grow bed. Put the second #14 o-ring over the threads of the male adapter, and attach the ½" female adapter. Hand tighten.

Step 9.

Place the water pump in the bottom of the fish tank, and then place the grow bed on top of the fish tank. Attach the ½" PVC pipe to the water pump and to the bottom of the ½" male adapter. You will have to measure the precise length based on your barrel and pump.

Step 10.

Attach a 9" length of ½" PVC pipe onto the female end of the adapter in the grow bed. Attach the ½" 90° elbow on top of the ½" pipe.

Step 11.

Cut a 6" piece of PVC pipe, and drill small holes in a line on one side. Start with a few, run your system, and add more as needed. Attach the pipe to the 90° elbow. Cap the pipe with the ½" end cap.

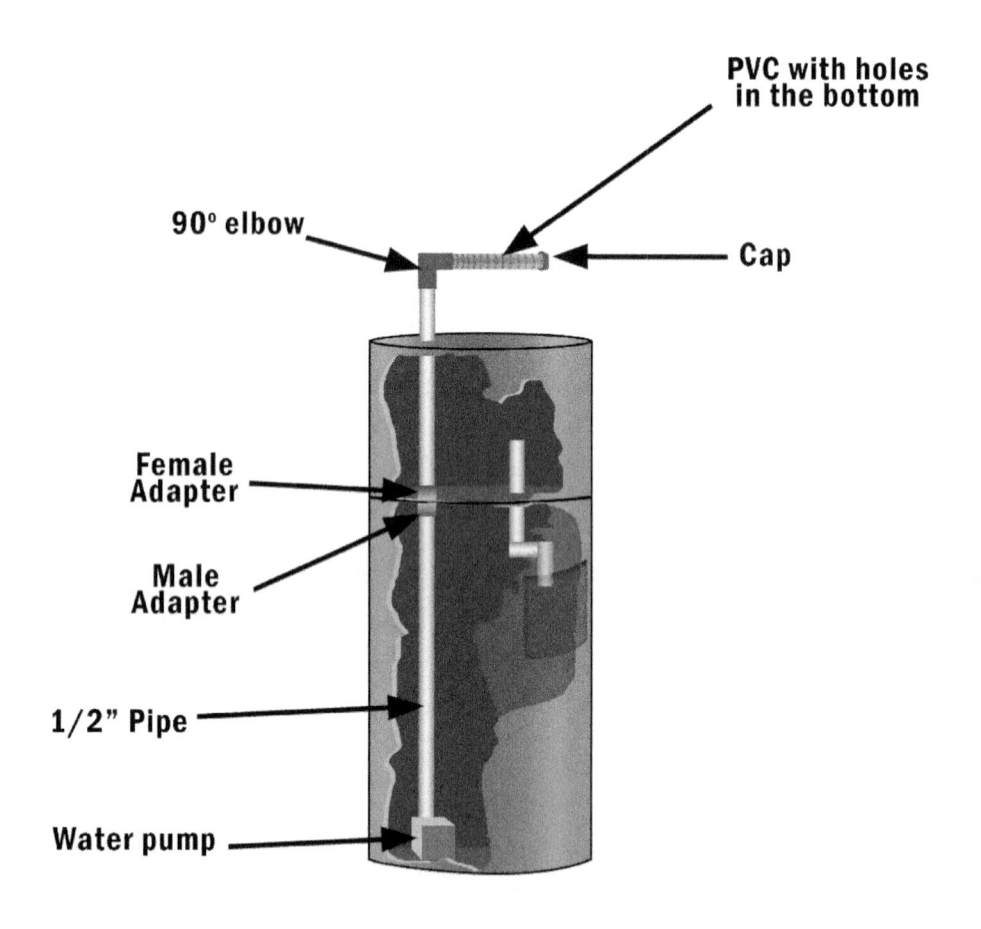

PVC with holes in the bottom

90° elbow

Cap

Female Adapter

Male Adapter

1/2" Pipe

Water pump

Step 12.

Use zip ties to attach the grow bed to the fish tank. Fill the fish tank with water.

Step 13.

Turn on the water pump, and check for leaks. The water should be pushed up the ½" pipe and out through the holes in the PVC in the top of the grow bed. As the water reaches the top of the bell siphon, the water should drain back into the fish tank.

Step 14.

If there are no leaks, rinse off the grow media, fill the grow bed with media, and begin to cycle your system.

IBC Totes

Pros	Cons
• IBC totes are easy to find for free	• Large, somewhat permanent
• Supports 10-20 fish	• Expensive if you have to buy an IBC tote
• Sturdy built-in frame	• Totes can leak from valves and caps

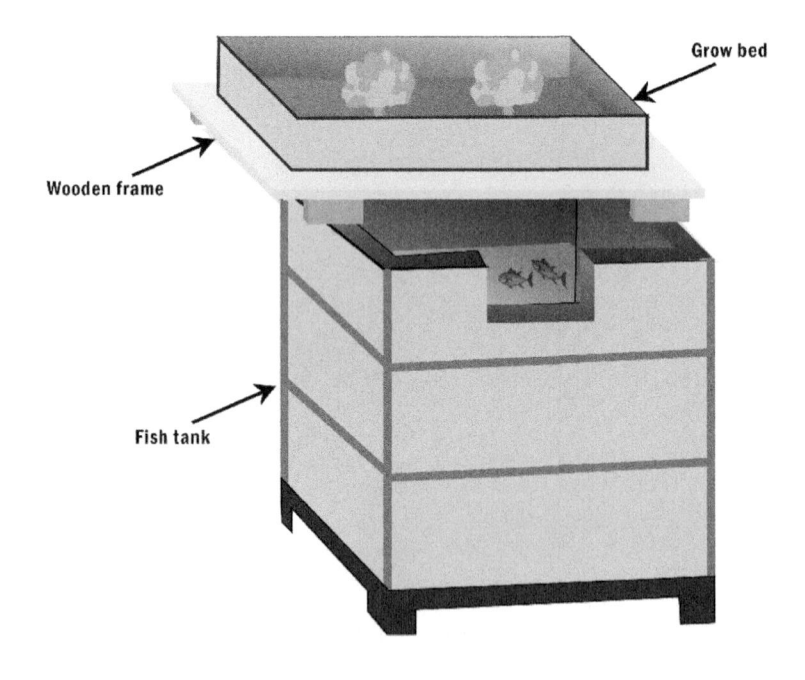

Labels: Grow bed, Wooden frame, Fish tank

This is by far the most popular aquaponic design. IBC totes are perfect for aquaponics, and they are fairly easy to find. Make sure the totes you use have only been used for food-safe products.

This IBC tote design will give you 16 sq' of grow bed area.

Materials:

- 48L" x 40W" x 46H" IBC tote **$250**
- Krylon Rust Protector spray paint **$6**
- 8- 6" flat corner braces & screws **$20**
- 2- 51" pieces of 2" x 6" hardwood planks **$10**
- 2- 37" pieces of 2" x 6" hardwood planks **$10**
- 790+ gallon/hour water pump **$70**
- 60" of 1" tubing to connect the water pump to the grow bed **$5**
- Adapter to attach 1" water pump tubing to water pump (size will depend on your water pump) **$5**
- Zip ties **$2**
- 2- 1" PVC valves **$4**
- 1- 1" t-fitting **$2**
- 2- 1" 90° fittings **$4**
- 14" length of 4" PVC pipe (media guard) **$2**
- 4" PVC cap (media guard) **$2**
- 1- ¾" to 1 ½" bell adapter (siphon) **$2**
- 2- 6" lengths of 1" PVC pipe (siphon, drain pipe) **$4**
- 1- 1" male threaded to slip adapter (siphon) **$2**
- 1- 1" female threaded to slip adapter (siphon) **$2**
- 2- #21 o-rings (siphon) **$3**

- 7 ¼" length of 2 ½" PVC pipe **$2**
- 1- 2 ½" PVC cap **$2**
- 2- 1" 90° PVC elbows **$5**
- Oil-based or marine-use paint. White or blue. **#30**
- Air stone **$20**
- 75-100 gallons of grow media

Total Estimated Cost: $464

Tools:

- Reciprocating saw
- Angle grinder
- Jigsaw
- Box cutter
- Drill
- Small drill bit
- Sandpaper
- Tool to cut plastic/pipe/tubing
- Permanent marker
- Paint brush

Directions[3]

Step 1.

Using a permanent marker, draw a line around the top of the tote right under the second horizontal cage piece (See illustration).

---
[3] System design from: https://www.howtoaquaponic.com/designs/ibc-aquaponics/

Cut all around the
cage right under this bar

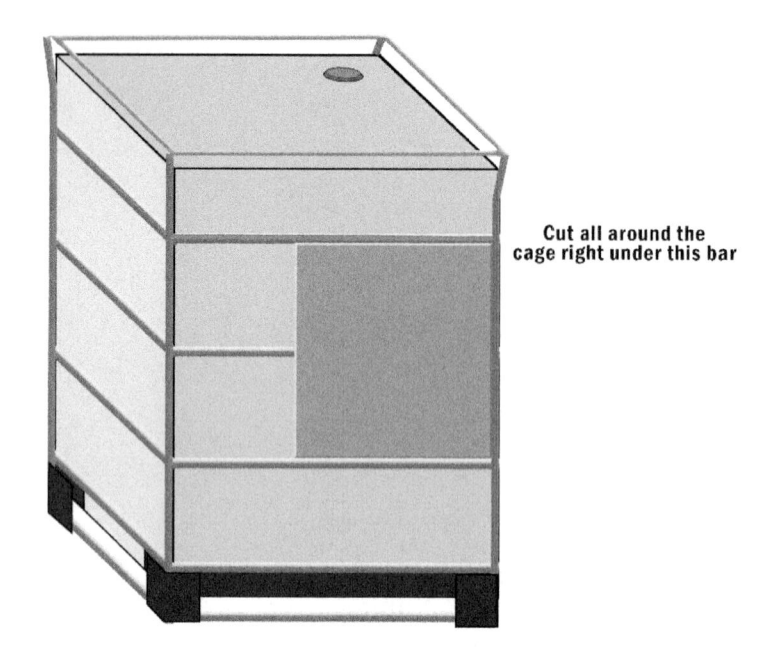

Step 2.

Remove the top bars from the cage, and save them for your grow bed. Tip over the cage and remove the tote. Unbolt the cage from the bottom frame.

Step 3.

Using a reciprocating saw, cut off the top of the cage. Cut around the cage under the top row of squares.

Step 4.

Use an angle grinder to smooth out the top of the bars on the fish tank (bottom) portion of the cage. Spray the cut edges with Krylon Rust Protector spray paint.

Step 5.

Cut off the top 14" of IBC tote with a jigsaw. This will become the grow bed. Cut around the IBC tote on the line that you drew in Step 1. This will leave a scrap piece of plastic, but it makes the fish tank easier to access and it lowers the grow bed to a manageable height.

Step 6.

Use sandpaper or a box cutter to clean the burrs off the cut edges of the IBC tote.

Step 7.

Flip the cage upside down into the base so that the painted rods of the cage set into the metal cage base. Cut out an access area for the fish from the short side of the cage (See illustrations).

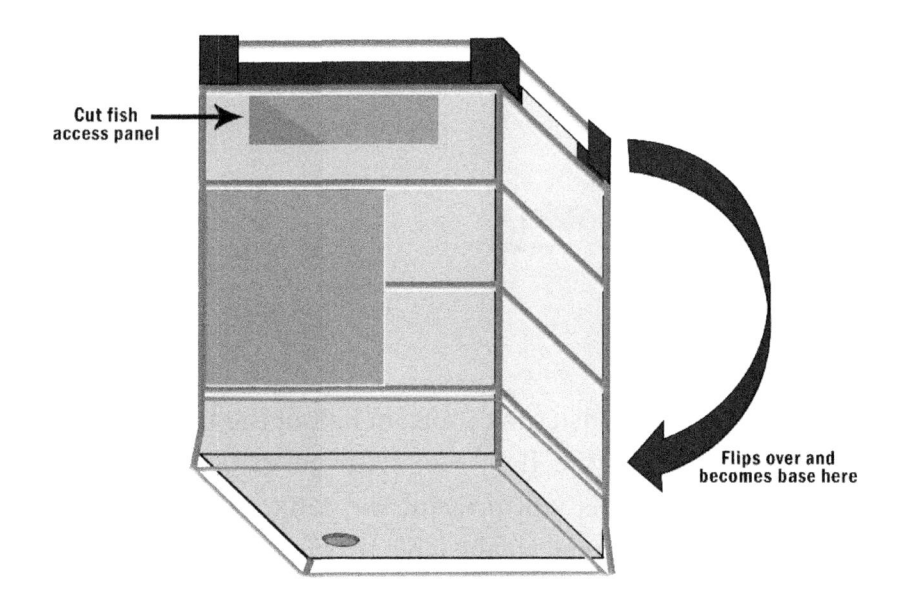

Step 8.

Use an angle grinder to clean up the cut cage edges, and spray with spray paint to prevent rust.

Step 9.

At this point, you should have the larger, bottom half of the metal cage sitting upside down on the metal base. The smaller, top end of the cage is the grow bed, and it should be with the top half of the IBC plastic tote.

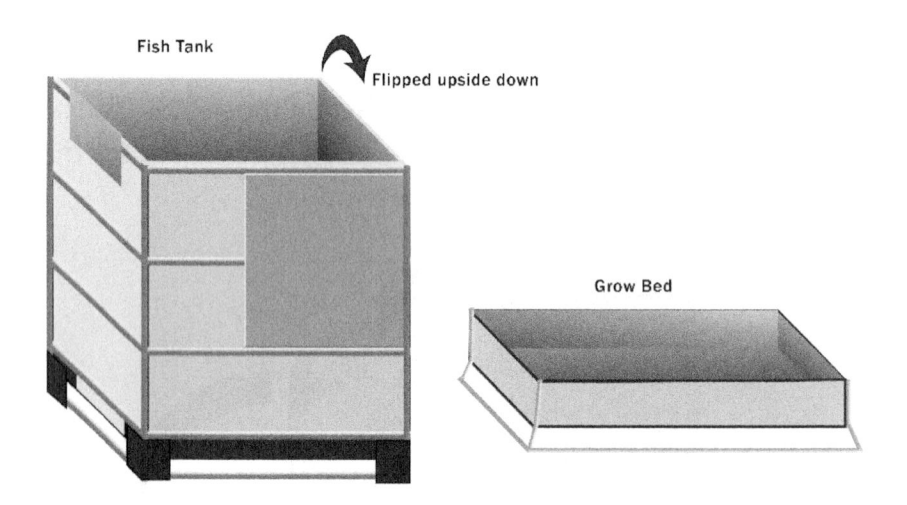

Step 10.

Paint the outside of the fish tank (bottom half of the IBC tote) and the grow bed (top half of the IBC tote) with an exterior oil-based or marine-grade paint. This will prevent the tank and grow bed from heating up, which can cause an algae bloom.

Step 10.

When dry, place the bottom half of the IBC tote inside the bottom half of the metal cage. This is the fish tank. The plastic tote should be lower than the edge of the cage. This will allow airflow between the fish tank and the grow bed.

Step 11.

Reattach the bars you removed in Step 2 to the top half of the metal cage.

Step 12.

Build a 43" x 51" square wooden frame from 2" x 6" hardwood planks. Reinforce the corners with metal corner brackets. The grow bed cage should sit squarely in the center of this frame when it is placed on top of the fish tank (See illustration).

Step 13.

Turn the frame 90° from the fish tank, and place it on top of the fish tank so that the long edge of the grow bed is resting across the short edge of the fish tank. Place the frame near the back of the fish tank so that the fish access cutout is in the front. Next, place the top half of the metal cage upside down on top of the wooden frame.

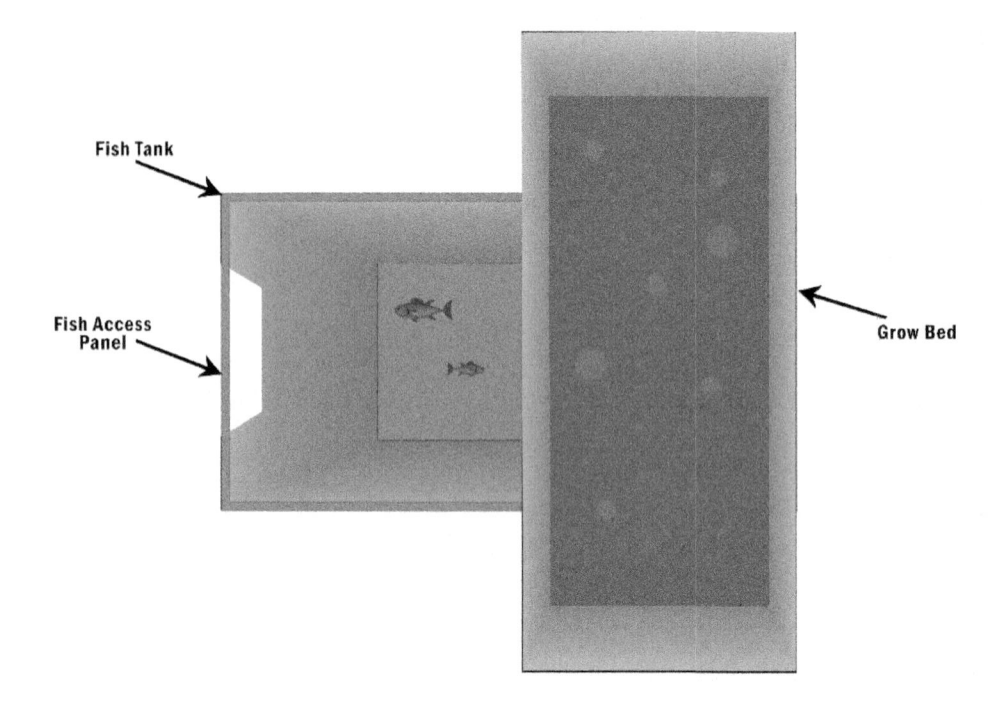

Step 14.

Cut off the plastic tabs that held the bars from the top half of the IBC tote. Use 100% silicone to seal the pressure release valve in the grow bed.

Step 15.

Use the adapter to connect the 1" water pump tubing to the water pump. Place the water pump into the fish tank.

Step 16.

Run the tubing up from the water pump until it is even with the top of the fish tank. Attach a 1" t-fitting. Use zip ties to hold it in place.

Step 17.

Attach a few inches of hose outward from the 90° section of the t-fitting, and attach a valve on the end. Use this valve to regulate water flow into the grow bed, and to add extra aeration into the system.

Step 18.

Attach more 1" tubing to the top of the t-fitting, and run it up from the fish tank to the bottom of the grow bed. Attach a valve, and then attach enough 1" tubing to reach the top of the grow bed. This valve will allow you to shut off the water in case you have a leak, and adjust the water flow rate into the grow bed.

Step 19.

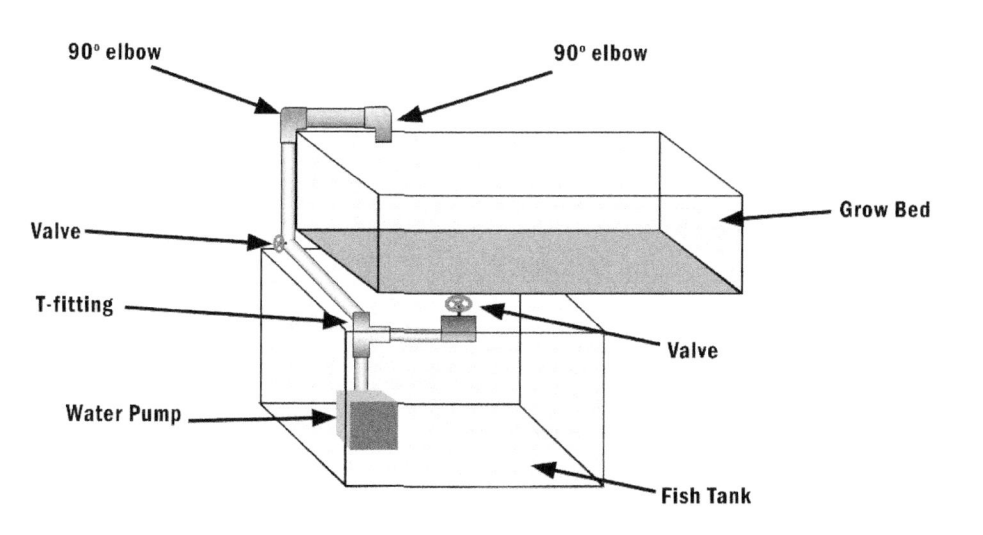

Attach a 90° fitting at the top of the tubing that fits over the top edge of the grow bed. Attach a few inches of 1" tubing, and then attach another 90° fitting. Use zip ties to hold it in place. This should result in tubing that comes up and over the edge of the grow bed and pumps water into the grow media.

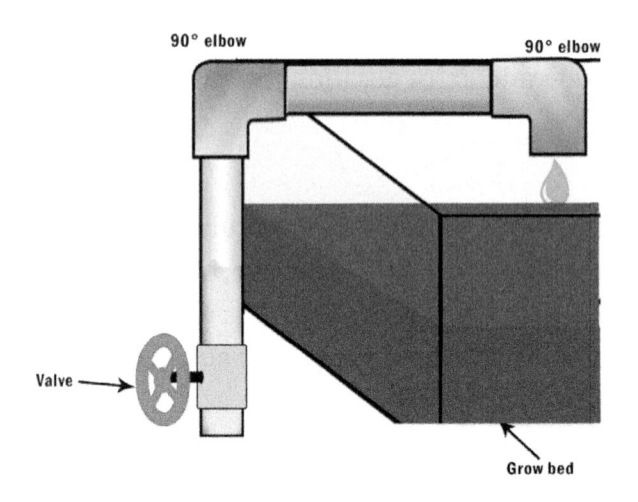

Step 20.

Use the 1" male threaded to slip adapter to trace a hole in the back right corner of the grow bed. Cut out the hole with a box cutter.

Step 21.

Make the bell siphon:

- Cut lines or drill holes into the 14" length of 4" PVC pipe to make the media guard (See illustration).

- Place a 4" cap on top of the media guard.

- Attach the ¾" to 1 ½" bell adapter to the 6" length of 1" PVC pipe.

- Attach the male threaded to slip adapter to the bottom of the 6" length of 1" PVC pipe.

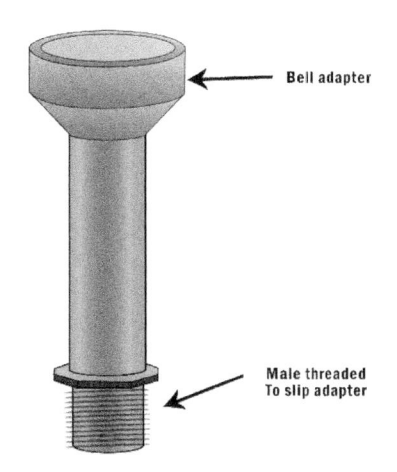

Bell adapter

Male threaded
To slip adapter

- Place an o-ring over the threads of the male adapter, and slip the threads through the hole in the back right corner of the grow bed.

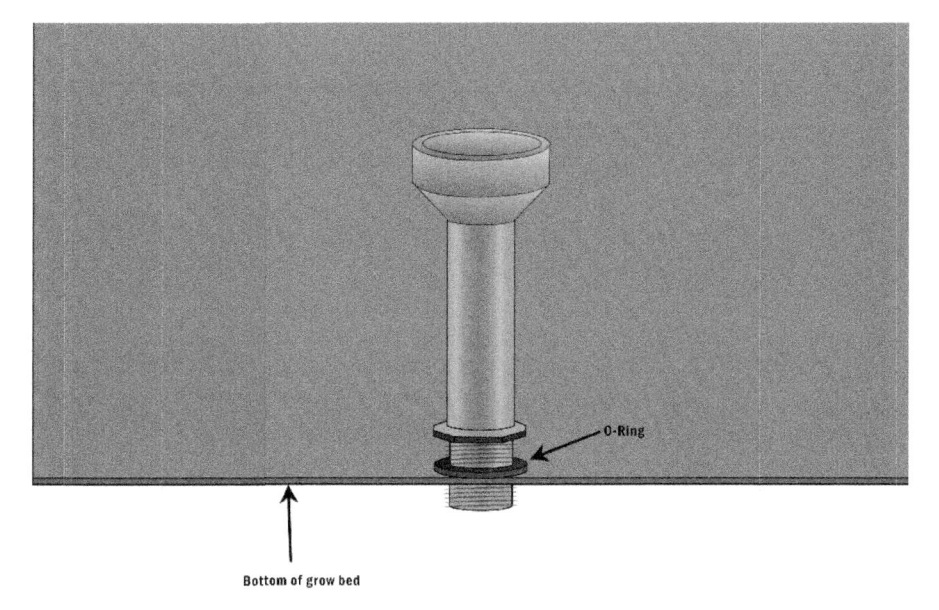

O-Ring

Bottom of grow bed

- Place another o-ring over the threads of the male adapter, and then screw on the 1" female threaded to slip adapter. This completes the siphon.

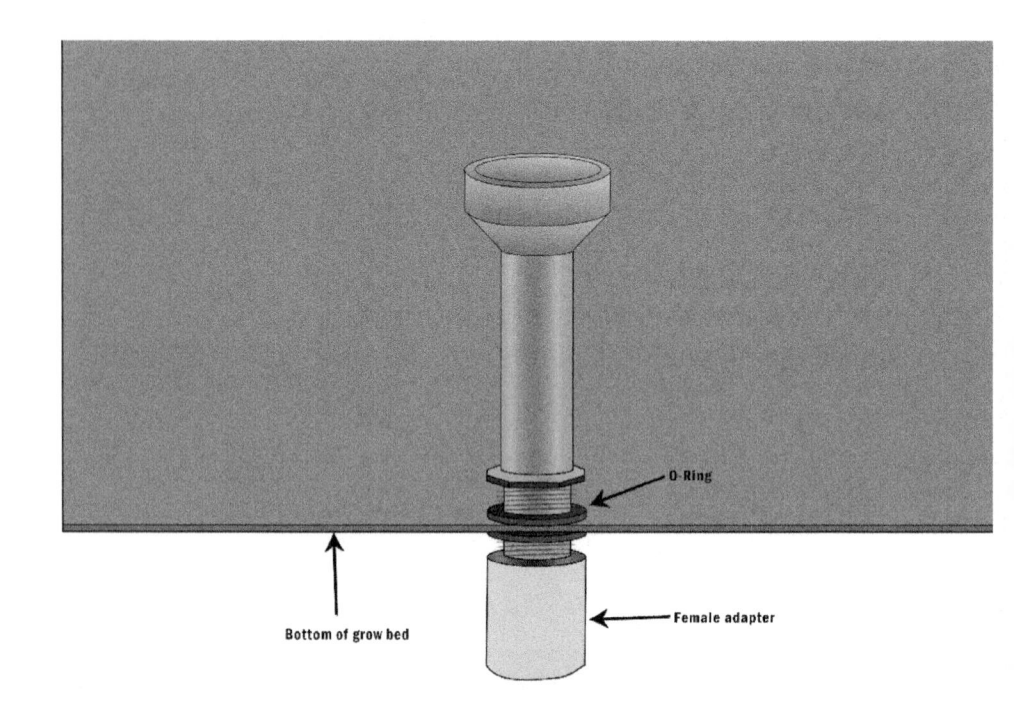

- Cut ½" notches into the bottom of the 7 ¼" length of 2 ½" PVC pipe (See illustration).

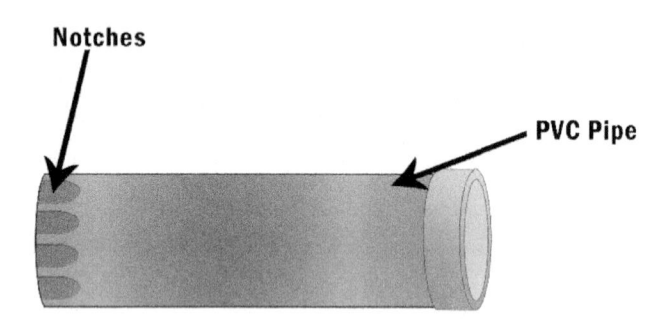

- Put the 2 ½" PVC cap on the top of the 7 ¼" length of 2 ½" PVC pipe. This is the bell.

- Place the bell over the siphon.
- Place the media guard over the bell.
- Attach a 1" 90° elbow to the bottom of the female threaded to slip adapter.
- Attach a 6" length of 1" PVC to the 90° elbow.
- Attach another 1" 90° elbow to the end of the 6" length of 1" PVC pipe.

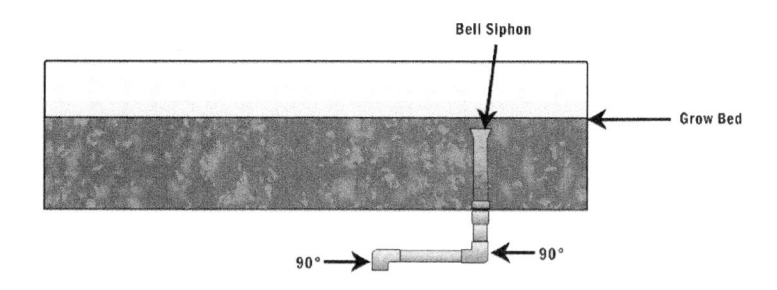

Step 22.

Rinse off the grow media thoroughly. Place the grow bed tote into the grow bed cage. Fill the grow bed with media, leaving at least 1" of space between the media and the edge of the grow bed.

Step 23.

Add an air stone into the fish tank.

Step 24.

Turn on the water pump. Check to make sure water flows up into the grow bed, and that the bell siphon drains it back into the fish tank. Check for leaks around the IBC valves and the bell siphon fittings. Use 100% silicone to seal any leaks in the tote, and use dope tape to fix leaks in the PVC pipe. Use valves to adjust water flow into the grow bed if the bell siphon is not draining properly.

Step 25.

Once the water is circulating appropriately, cycle your system.

Each of these systems omits the need for a sump tank because the grow bed sits directly on top of the fish tank. This reduces the amount of space the system will use, and it also reduces the amount of plumbing to build and clean.

You can scale any system up or down as long as you keep a 1:1 ratio of fish tank volume to grow bed volume. However, while these designs can be scaled up, DWC systems are best for large operations.

Alex Francis Pro/Shutterstock.com

Deep-Water Culture

Deep-water culture systems are easy to modify and customize. Basic DWC systems are best for beginners who want to work towards a profitable setup.

Deep-water culture aquaponic systems (DWC) are best for large-scale hobby operations. They are more difficult to build, but much easier to work with. The beds are also lighter and easier to customize. However, due to a lack of grow media, this system needs an extra biofilter and may need added nutrients for some crops.

Deep-channel systems can be either flood-and-drain or continuous flow.

Continuous flow systems are more popular, and utilize rafts that float on top of the grow beds to hold plants. The major benefits of this system are that the fish have a consistent level of water in the tank, and the water has more contact with the bacteria that break down waste.

Flood-and-drain systems can be more difficult to maintain, since the roots will be exposed to open air each time the grow bed drains. If the system isn't timed correctly, the roots can dry out and kill the plants. These systems use a solid frame over the grow bed with holes to hold the plants.

Pros:	Cons:
• Easy to plant and harvest	• Unable to support fruiting plants
• More stable water temperatures	• More filters required
• More stable pH values	• Higher cost to heat or cool water
• Larger margin of error for maintenance	• Up to 75% more fish feed required
• Faster plant growth	• Additional aeration methods

Floats/Rafts/Frames

Instead of a growing media, deep-channel systems use either a fixed or floating structure to hold plants in place. Floats and frames will have holes cut into them to hold netted pots filled with rockwool, growing media, or both.

In a continuous-flow system, floating rafts can support plants on top of the water. In a flood-and-drain system, the grow beds will be empty frequently, which requires a solid support frame on top of the grow bed.

Floats/Rafts

Rafts are the lightest and easiest plant support structure to work with. They can be moved for planting and harvesting, and taken out for maintenance on the system. Use a plywood template with holes cut the appropriate size and distance to make cutting your rafts easier and more consistent.

Rafts are constructed using lightweight, buoyant material. These materials are usually inexpensive and easy to find:

Pros/Cons	XPS (Extruded Polystyrene)	EPS (Expanded Polystyrene)	Corrugated Plastic (Twinwall)
Water Resistance	High	Moderate	High
UV Resistance	Low	Low	High
Durability	Moderate	Low	High
Buoyancy	High	High	Low
Estimated Cost per sq'	$1.10	$.75	$1.60

XPS

Extruded polystyrene is the most widely-used material for aquaponic rafts. It is more durable than EPS, and cheaper than corrugated plastic. Foam should be 2" thick to support mature plants. Extruded polystyrene is usually found in the insulation section of hardware stores, and can be blue, pink, or green. Do not use foam with plastic or foil liners.

The only problem with XPS is that it has a very low UV resistance, which means it will fall apart in an outdoor system. Growers solve this by painting the top of the XPS board with non-toxic paint. This also helps prolong the life of the foam; you can expect 2-3 growing seasons out of painted XPS board.

Paint that is safe for aquaponic systems must meet the following requirements:

- Must be labeled "For use in potable containers" or "Food safe"
- Must be designed for use on plastic
- Must *not* be mildew-resistant or mold-resistant
- Must be fully cured before coming in contact with the water

The most common paint used inside aquariums is Krylon Fusion spray paint. Apply at least two coats to the top of your foam board, and allow it to cure completely. Rinse the boards thoroughly before introducing them to your system.

EPS

Expanded polystyrene is used for rafts that will support small plants. EPS is the white, crumbly foam that is used for packaging, and it falls apart quickly in an aquaponic system. However, it is a much cheaper option than XPS, which makes it a popular choice for many growers.

Three ways to improve the durability of EPS are:

- Use 2"-thick foam
- Cut the foam into smaller, 2'x2' sections
- Paint the top of each foam section

Expanded polystyrene can last 1-2 growing seasons if it is handled gently and used with small plants, like leafy greens and herbs. Once

EPS starts crumbling, remove it from the system. Those little white crumbles will clog pipes and filters.

Expanded polystyrene sheets are white, and are usually found in the insulation section of a hardware store. Do not use sheets with a plastic or foil liner.

Corrugated Plastic

Although this material has the most potential for long-term rafts, it is not widely used. Corrugated plastic is exactly like corrugated cardboard; the ends of the material are open to show the fluted material in the middle. In order for the plastic sheet to be buoyant, these ends must be sealed.

Corrugated plastic is also the most expensive option; over twice the cost of EPS foam board.

If the ends are not completely sealed, the air pockets will fill with water and the board will sink. The ends can be sealed with 100% pure silicone (no anti-mold or mildew additives), and added to the system once the silicone is fully cured. You can also melt the ends of the board with a torch. Test a sealed board by submerging it in water and checking for air bubbles.

Frames

In a flood-and-drain system, permanent frames with holes cut into them support the plants. As water drains from the grow bed, the roots will be exposed to open air. If a frame does not cover the majority of the growing area, the roots will be exposed to light, drafts, and possible contaminants. This limits most frame designs to some sort of rigid, waterproof board placed over the grow bed.

Materials for building a frame must meet the same requirements as all other plastics within the system. Plastics marked with a 1, 2, 4, and 5 SPI codes are food-safe and non-toxic for plants and fish. Some plastics with an SPI code of 7 are also safe, but you should do more research before adding it to your system.

Plant Support

Deep-water aquaponic systems use a variety of methods for holding the plants upright in floats or frames:

Pros/Cons	Rockwool	Netted Pots	Growing Media
Durable	High	Moderate	High
Stable	High	Low	Moderate
Porous	High	Low	Moderate
Reusable		X	X
Estimated Cost per plant (2")	$.20-$.50	$.40-$.50	Varies

Pots

The size of the hole you cut into floats and frames will be determined by the plants you want to grow. Short, leafy greens can sit in small pots with relative stability. Tall, top-heavy plants will need larger pots to keep them from tipping over.

The pots should be slightly larger than the hole cut into the raft or frame. This will allow the pot to fit snugly without falling through.

Netted pots have slits cut into the sides to allow the roots to grow down towards the water. Many hobby growers make their own out of yogurt containers, plastic cups, and other recycled materials. There are also commercially-available hydroponic netted cups that are more stable, but also more costly.

Pots will be filled with either rockwool, growing media, or both. If seeds are germinated in a rockwool cube, the cube can be directly transplanted into a netted pot. Growing media can be poured around the rockwool to add stability, but this is not necessary for smaller plants.

Rockwool

Rockwool was originally used as insulation, but has become the primary growing media in hydroponics and aquaponics. Basalt is melted down into a liquid, and spun like cotton candy into a fibrous block. The block is then formed into cubes, and holes are pressed into the top for seeds.

Rockwool blocks are incredibly porous, which helps them trap nutrients as water flows through. Seeds can be directly planted into blocks, and then transplanted into netted pots.

Soak cubes in a tub before planting seeds and wait until all the air bubbles have escaped, which signals that the block is thoroughly saturated. Allow the blocks to drain, but do not wring out excess water. Plant seeds into the blocks, and keep them in a seed-starting tray with a humidity dome until germination.

The major disadvantage of using rockwool is the cost per cube, considering they are not reusable.

Growing Media

Growing media can be used to support a rockwool cube inside a netted pot, or as a replacement for rockwool inside a netted pot. Heavier grow media offers more stability, which is why clay pebbles and river rock are the most popular media choices for deep-channel production.

If you decide not to use rockwool, you will need to germinate seeds in a seed-starting plug or sponge. Seeds planted directly into growing media will wash through, so they need extra support until the root system can spread out.

Hydroponic supply companies sell many seed-starting plugs, but many are made from organic materials. These materials can affect pH and nutrients, and can clog the system as they break down. Synthetic plugs and sponges can give seedlings support until they grow through the media. For small systems, you can cut your own plugs from cheap household sponges.

Grow Beds

DWC grow beds are similar to media-filled beds, except they aren't filled with media. Most DWC systems use a continuous-flow circulation method, so water is constantly circulating through the system.

Grow beds for DWC systems can be shallower than media-filled beds, but this will also limit plant selection. DWC systems are best for leafy greens, herbs, and small fruiting vegetables, because they have smaller root systems and require less nutrition.

Fish & Fish Tanks

Remember; fish waste feeds the bacteria in your system, which in turn feeds the plants. Media-filled beds provide a large amount of biological surface area (BSA) for bacteria to colonize, which gives them the ability to transform large amounts of waste.

DWC systems don't have the same amount of grow media, which can make it more difficult for bacteria to do their jobs. This can result in a system that is unable to support a high stocking density because the bacteria can't keep up with the waste. When you choose fish for a DWC system, select fish that thrive in a low to medium stocking density, and like slightly cooler water temperatures.

The material for a fish tank should meet the same standards as the materials for the rest of your system. Deep tanks are preferable to shallow tanks because they maintain water temperature easier, and give fish a more comfortable habitat.

Plumbing & Filtration

Most DWC systems are continuous-flow with a solids filter and BSA filter. The solids filter allows solid waste to settle out of the system, which gives bacteria the chance to mineralize the waste and release nutrients. The BSA filter provides a large surface area for nitrifying bacteria to transform ammonia into nitrogen.

The solids filter is usually placed after the fish tank and before the grow beds, while the BSA filter can be anywhere in the system, but usually comes after the grow bed and before the fish tank. Healthy filters are vital to the health of your aquaponic system, so make sure your filters are large enough to handle the amount of waste your fish will produce. This will also help your system support a higher stocking density, which will result in a higher nutrient content.

A deep-water culture system will be more complex to build, but it is much easier to scale up for a variety of growing goals. Luckily, many of the materials are easy to find for free.

Building a DWC System

Deep-water culture aquaponic systems work best for growers who want to specialize in certain crops, and who want to have a larger fish harvest. These systems are more versatile with their setup, but they do require external filtration to make up for the BSA lost by not having a grow media.

Make sure all materials used in your system meet the requirements laid out in the deep-water culture chapter.

A basic DWC aquaponic system is made up of the following components:

- Fish Tank
- Aerator
- Water Pump
- Grow Bed
- Siphons
- BSA filter
- Solids filter
- Timer
- Sump Tank
- Plumbing

There is one simple DWC system that can be scaled up to meet the demands of a small profitable operation. IBC totes are the easiest building material for these systems, although the design can be modified to use stock tanks or plastic-lined frames with the same volume.

DWC IBC Tote System

Pros	Cons
• Profitable system	• Difficult for indoor use
• IBC totes are easy to find for free	• System is nearly permanent
• Lower cost than similar-sized media bed system	• Less crop variety

IBC totes are the most popular aquaponic system material. It is easy to find them for free, and they come with a built-in supportive cage. Find IBC totes that have been used for food-safe materials to prevent toxic chemicals in your system.

Materials:

- 3- IBC totes **$750**
- 2- 55-gallon plastic barrels **$100**
- 30' of 1" PVC pipe **$9**
- 25' of 1" flexible tubing **$30**

- 25' of 8mm plastic tubing **$10**
- Zip ties **$5**
- 40 cinder blocks **$52**
- Swirl Filter Materials
    - 3-1" male threaded to slip adapters
    - 3- 1" female threaded to slip adapters
    - 6- #21 o-rings
    - 1- 1" t-fitting (swirl filter) **$2**
    - 2- 1" 90° PVC elbows (swirl filter) **$4**
    - 1- 1" PVC valve (swirl filter) **$2**
- Biofilter Materials
    - 2- 1" male threaded to slip adapters
    - 2- 1" female to threaded slip adapters
    - 4- #21 o-rings
    - 1- 1" t-fitting **$2**
    - 2- 1" PVC caps **$4**
- Drain Pipe Materials
    - 3- 1" barrel connectors **$6**
    - 3- 1" female adaptors **$6**
    - 1- 1" PVC elbow **$2**
    - 2- 1" female PVC t-fittings **$4**
    - 3- 1" rubber washers **$3**

- 1- 1" male threaded to slip adapter
- 1- 1" female threaded to slip adapter
- 2- #21 o-rings
- 1- 1" PVC elbow **$2**
- Connecting biofilter to fish tank and grow beds
  - 1,000gph+ submersible water pump (with a lift of at least 4') **$100**
  - 3- 1" t-fittings **$6**
  - 4- 1" valves **$8**
  - 4- 1" 90° elbows **$8**
- Air pump and air stones.
  - 1,000-gallon+ air pump **$125**
  - 4- air stones **$10**
  - 3-8mm barbed t-connectors **$5**
  - 1- 8mm 90° barbed elbow **$2**
- 1- 1" male threaded to slip adapter
- 1- 1" female threaded to slip adapter
- 2- #21 o-rings
- Bio balls
- Plastic sponge or mesh for the biofilter
- Enough floating raft material to cover 3 grow beds

Total Cost: $1,297

Tools:

- Drill
- Small drill bit (¼"-3/8")
- Jigsaw
- PVC glue
- 100% silicone
- Caulk gun
- Dope tape
- Measuring tape

Directions[4]

Step 1.

Remove the bars on the top of one IBC tote. Use a jigsaw to cut out the top of the IBC tote. This will be the fish tank. Place the fish tank on top of 4 evenly-spaced cinder blocks.

Step 2.

Build the swirl filter:

- Drill a 1" hole 2/3 of the way up one 55-gallon barrel.

---

[4] System design plans: http://www.fao.org/3/CA2549EN/ca2549en.pdf

- Drill another 1" hole 90° to the right of the first hole, and a few inches higher.
- Attach the male and female threaded to slip adapters together through the hole with o-rings between them.
- Drill a third 1" hole at the bottom of the barrel.
- Attach the male and female threaded to slip adapters together through the first hole with o-rings between them. Attach a 4" length of 1" PVC on the inside of the barrel, and a t-fitting on the end.
- Attach a 3" length of 1" PVC on each side of the t-fitting.
- Attach a 1" 90° elbow on the end of each 3" length of 1" PVC pipe.
- Attach the male and female threaded to slip adapters with o-rings on each side to the bottom hole. Attach a 1" length of 1" PVC on the outside of the barrel.
- Attach a 1" valve to the 1" PVC pipe.

Step 3:

Build the biofilter:

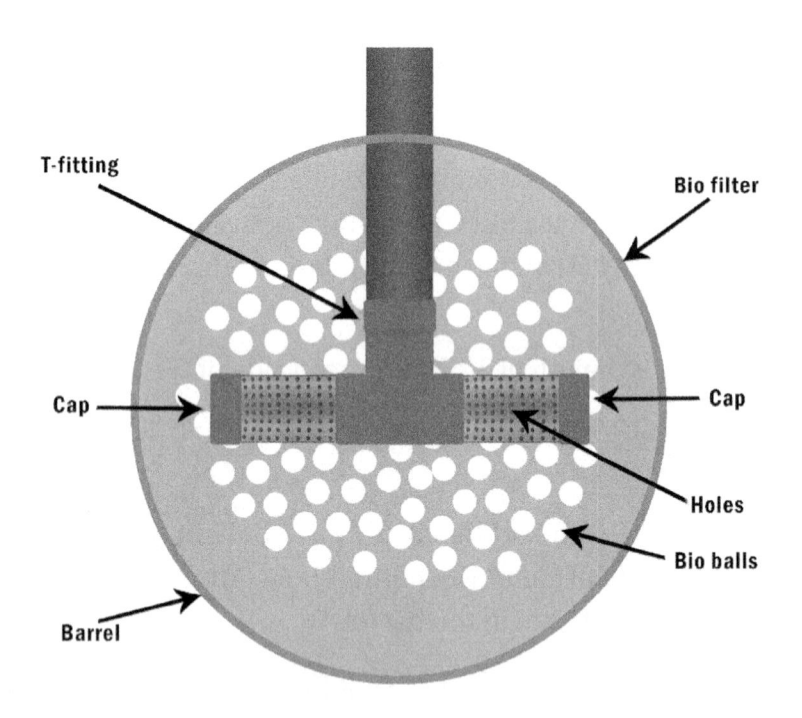

Figure: Biofilter diagram showing T-fitting, Bio filter, Cap (both sides), Holes, Bio balls, and Barrel.

- Drill a 1" hole at the same height as the 2nd (higher) 1" hole in the swirl filter.
- Connect a male and female threaded to slip adapters together through the hole with o-rings between them. Attach a 4" length of 1" PVC on the inside adapter.
- Connect the higher hole in the swirl filter to the biofilter with a short length of 1" PVC pipe attached to the adapters.
- Attach a 1" t-fitting to the end of the 4" length of 1" PVC.
- Cut 2 pieces of 3" long 1" PVC pipe.

- Drill small holes in the 2 pieces of PVC pipe.
- Attach the two pieces on both sides of the 1" t-fitting.
- Attach 1" caps on the ends of both pieces of PVC. You may need to glue these caps on.

Step 4.

Use a permanent marker to mark under the first horizontal metal cage piece on 2 IBC totes.

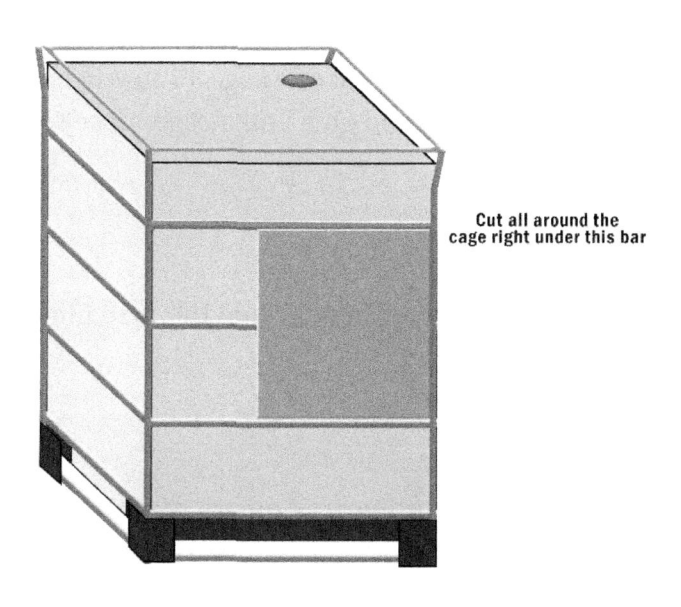

Cut all around the cage right under this bar

Step 5.

Remove the top bars from the metal cages of the 2 IBC totes with permanent marker. Remove the totes from the cages.

Step 6.

Use a jigsaw to cut off the tops of both IBC totes along the permanent marker lines. This should give you 2 grow beds approximately 12" deep.

Step 7.

Use a reciprocating saw to cut the first row of squares off the tops of both metal cages and the bottom of one cage. (You will have to remove the base to do this). This should give you a cage piece to hold each of the grow beds.

Step 8.

Place the plastic IBC tote grow beds inside the matching cage pieces. These are the grow beds.

Step 9.

Use cinder blocks to build supporting pillars for the grow beds. Make 4 pillars 3 blocks high in a square so that the corners of the grow beds sit squarely in the center of the blocks. Place the 3 beds in a row with a few inches in between each bed. The bed closest to the fish tank will be Bed A, the middle bed will be Bed B, and the bed farthest from the fish tank will be Bed C.

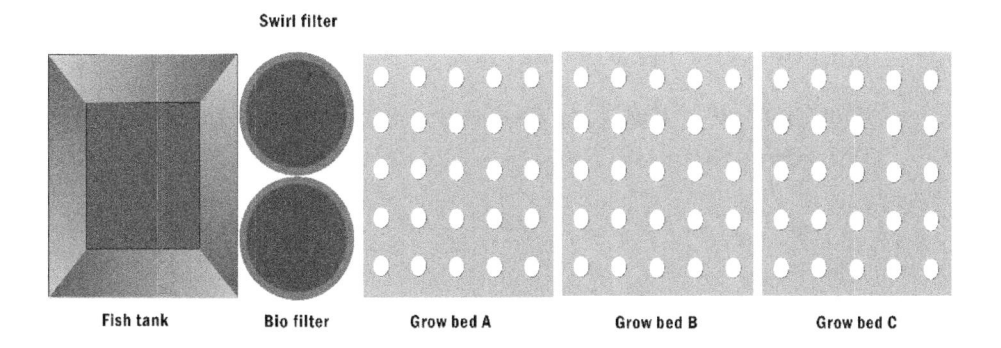

Fish tank   **Swirl filter**   **Bio filter**   **Grow bed A**   **Grow bed B**   **Grow bed C**

Step 10.

Build the drain pipes:

- Drill a 1" hole close to the center in the bottom of each grow bed. If there is a cap or valve in the IBC tote, use 100% silicone to seal it.
- In each bed, place a rubber washer inside the grow bed on the 1" hole, and connect a barrel connector and tighten.
- Place a female adapter onto the barrel connector inside each grow bed.
- Cut 3 10" pieces of 1" PVC pipe.
- Place one 10" pipe into each female adapter inside each grow bed.
- Place the female PVC elbow on the bottom of the barrel connector on the outside of Bed C.
- Place a female PVC t-fitting on the bottom of the barrel connectors on the outside of Bed B and Bed A.

- Cut enough 1" PVC pipe to connect the elbow underneath Bed C to the t-fitting on Bed B.
- Cut enough 1" PVC pipe to connect the t-fitting underneath Bed B to the t-fitting on Bed A.

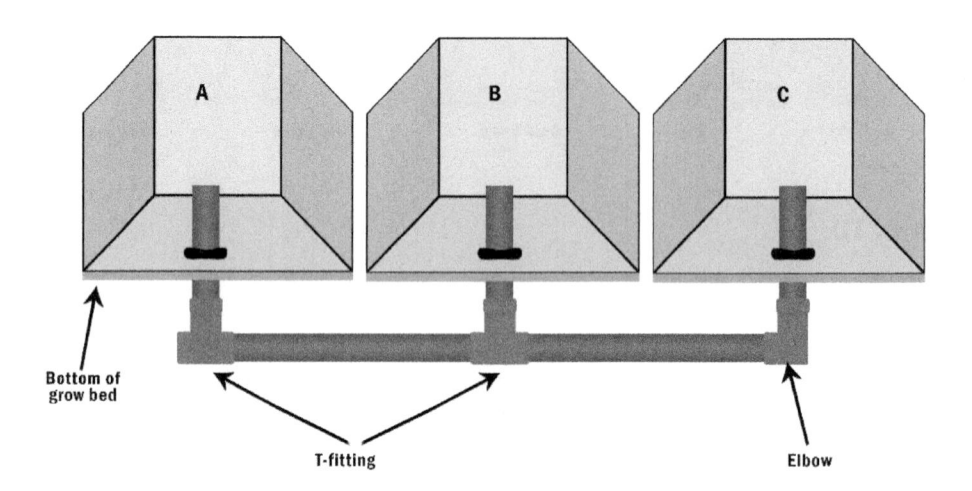

![Diagram showing three grow beds A, B, C connected by PVC pipe with t-fittings and an elbow at the bottom. Labels: Bottom of grow bed, T-fitting, Elbow.]

- Drill a 1" hole in the biofilter 45° to the left of the top hole. Make sure this hole will sit 6" lower than the top of the stand pipes in the grow beds.
- Connect a male and female threaded to slip adapter through the new hole in the biofilter. Use an o-ring between them.
- Connect a 1" PVC elbow to the adapter.
- Cut enough 1" PVC pipe to connect the t-fitting underneath Bed A to the PVC elbow.

Step 11.

Connect the biofilter to the grow beds and fish tank.

- Place the water pump in the bottom of the biofilter.
- Use an adapter to connect 1" flexible tubing to the water pump.
- Cut the tubing a few inches above the top of the biofilter barrel.
- Attach a 1" t-fitting to the top of the tubing.
- Connect 1" flexible tubing to the t-fitting, and measure out enough to reach over the lip of the fish tank.
- Use zip ties to hold the tubing to the cage of the fish tank.
- Attach a 1" valve to the end of the tubing to control flow.
- Connect 1" flexible tubing to the other side of the t-fitting, and measure the tubing to the closest corner of Bed A. Cut the tubing, and connect it to the cage with zip ties.
- Attach a 1" t-fitting to the tubing.
- Connect a 1" valve to leg of the t-fitting that points towards the inside of the grow bed.
- Connect a 1" 90° elbow to the valve so the water will spray down into the bed.
- Connect 1" flexible tubing to the remaining leg of the t-fitting, and measure the tubing to the closest corner of Bed B. Cut the tubing, and connect it to the cage with zip ties.
- Attach a 1" t-fitting, 1" valve, and 90° elbow like Bed A.

- Connect 1" flexible tubing to the remaining leg of the t-fitting, and measure the tubing to the closest corner of Bed C. Cut the tubing, and connect it to the cage with zip ties.
- Attach a 1" 90° elbow to the tubing.
- Attach a 1" valve to the elbow.
- Attach a 1" 90° elbow to the valve.

Step 12.

Install the air pump and air stones.

- Attach the air pump to the highest point of the system; likely the outside edge of the fish tank.
- Attach a short length of 8mm tubing to the air pump, and then attach a barbed t-connector.
- Run a length of 8mm tubing from the t-connector to the nearest corner of Bed A.
- Attach the tubing to the sides of the grow beds with zip ties.
- Attach a barbed t-connector to the tubing.
- Drill an 8mm (5/16") hole in the top edge of Bed A.

Barbed Tubing

Clear Tubing

Hole in the wall on the top of the grow bed

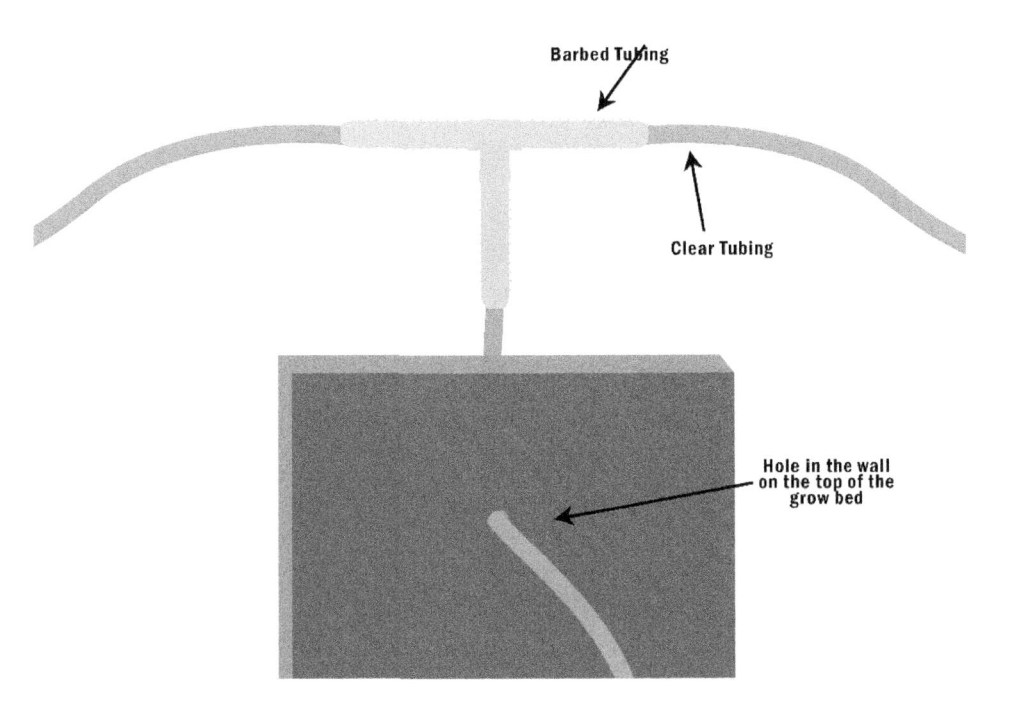

- Attach enough tubing to reach from the t-connector to an air stone in the bottom of the grow bed.
- Attach tubing to the t-connector, and measure enough to reach the nearest corner of Bed B.
- Using the same method, install an air stone.
- Attach tubing to the t-connector, and measure enough to reach the nearest corner of Bed C.
- Use the same method to install an air stone, except use a barbed 90° connector for the final air stone.
- Drill an 8mm hole in the top of the fish tank.
- Attach tubing to the t-connector near the air pump, and measure enough tubing to reach the bottom of the tank.

Attach an air stone to the tubing, and set the air stone in the bottom of the fish tank.

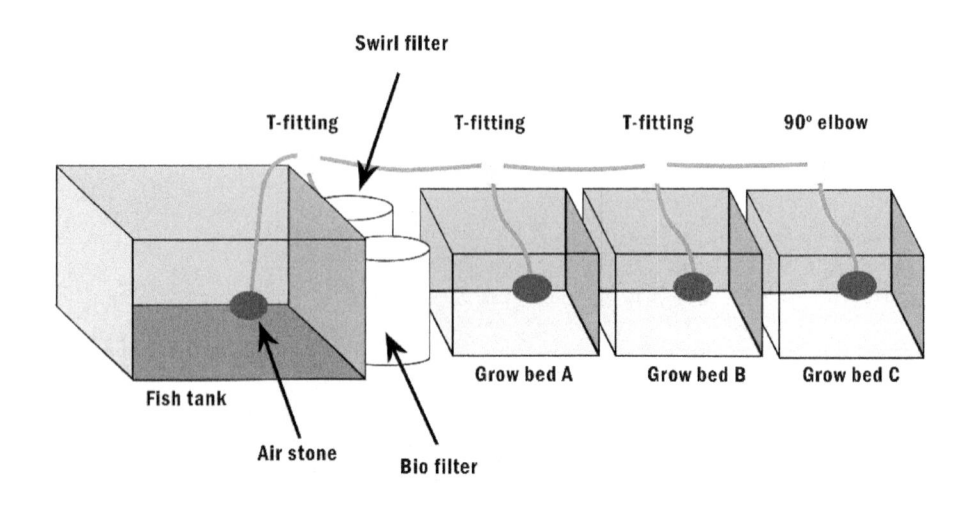

Swirl filter, T-fitting, T-fitting, T-fitting, 90° elbow, Fish tank, Air stone, Bio filter, Grow bed A, Grow bed B, Grow bed C

Step 13.

Drill a 1" hole in the fish tank at the same height as the first (lower) 1" hole in the swirl filter. Make sure this hole is on the same side as the grow beds.

Step 14.

Attach a male and female threaded to slip adapter through the hole in the fish tank. Use o-rings between them.

Step 15.

Cut a length of 1" PVC pipe long enough to connect the fish tank to the swirl filter.

Step 16.

Fill the biofilter with plastic bio balls and place a layer of sponge or mesh on top to keep the balls in place. Leave a few inches of space between the media and the PVC pipe.

Step 17.

Build the rafts.

- Cut your floating raft material to fit into the grow beds. Leave some space to reach under the material if you need to lift it out, but try to cover as much of the surface area of the water as possible.
- Cut holes into the raft material that will fit netted pots or rockwool.
- Cut holes for the center standpipe in each grow bed.

Step 18.

Fill the entire system with water. Plug in and turn on the water pump and air pump. Adjust the valves on the grow beds to make sure 20% of the water is pumped into the grow beds, and 80% of the water is pumped back into the fish tank. Check for leaks, and adjust PVC fittings with dope tape if needed. Use 100% silicone to seal any other leaks.

Step 19.

Once the system is running smoothly, begin the cycling process.

While this system uses IBC totes for the fish tank and grow beds, stock tanks, plastic-lined wooden frames, and many other materials can be substituted. The plumbing will be similar in any model, although the types of fittings and measurements will necessarily change.

Once your system is up and running, you will need to do consistent maintenance for healthy fish and plants.

Maintenance & Troubleshooting

An aquaponic system requires consistent testing and maintenance to keep your fish and plants healthy.

Task	Daily	Weekly	As-Needed
Feeding Fish	X		
Checking Water Temp.	X		
Water Testing		X	
pH Testing		X	
Fish Harvest			X
Plant Harvest			X
Seed Starting			X

Proper maintenance is the key to a healthy system. Most issues with an aquaponic system can be resolved with consistent tests and adjustments before harmful conditions cause a system crash.

Maintenance

An aquaponic system requires more maintenance than a traditional vegetable garden. It is impossible to leave an aquaponic system unattended for even one day. If you must go out of town, ask a trusted friend to take over the maintenance requirements for a few days.

Feeding Fish

Your fish will need fed every day. The amount you feed will depend on the life stage and species of fish in your tank.

A general rule is to feed no more than the fish will eat in five minutes. If you notice extra feed floating in the system, cut back gradually until you reduce your waste to no more than 5%.

The fish will only produce nutrient-rich waste if they eat nutrient-rich food. Ask your fish supplier for the best fish feed for your species of fish. Cheap fish feed may result in low amounts of nutrients.

Water Temperature

The water in your fish tank should not fluctuate more than 3° per day in either direction. Large fluctuations can stress your fish, which can lead to lower activity and disease.

Aim for a temperature that fits your fish and your plants, and try to maintain that temperature throughout the year. This is easier in an indoor system, but it's possible in some outdoor systems in certain climates.

It is always easier to heat water than it is to cool it down, so try to design your system around warm-weather thresholds rather than cool-weather thresholds. A hoophouse can help maintain warmer air temperatures for plants during winter months. Shade cloth or canopies can prevent the water temperature from climbing during the summer.

Record the water temperature at the same time every day. Gradual declines are fine as long as they remain within the healthy range for the fish. A log of daily temperatures will help you determine how your system responds to weather patterns, which will help you plan in the future.

Water Testing

You should try to test your water once per week. A basic freshwater aquarium test should show the ammonia levels of your water, and a hydroponic water test will check basic nutrients.

Keep a log of your test results each week so you can compare temperature fluctuations to nutrient fluctuations. You should also record any activity that may impact results, like a water change or harvesting large amounts of plants or fish.

Plants are fairly tolerant of nutrient fluctuations, so you want to avoid amending the water with a specific nutrient unless the plants show signs of deficiency. Wait to see if the pH, temperature, or fish feed may be causing nutrient problems and make adjustments there before adding new chemicals to your system.

pH Testing

The pH levels of your system will determine how much of each nutrient is available to your plants. Too low or too high, and certain nutrients become deficient or toxic very quickly.

The balance between the ideal pH for plants and the ideal pH for fish can be difficult to maintain. Nitrification lowers pH, while denitrification raises it. Adding new water can raise or lower pH, and sometimes a pH imbalance seems to come from nowhere.

Plants and fish can tolerate pH values outside of their ideal range as long as they happen gradually. If your pH is too low or too high, you can use an amendment to raise or lower your pH. However, you will want to do this slowly, and try to adjust the value by no more than .3 points per day.

Keep a log of the pH each time you test. This data, along with your temperature and nutrient logs, can help you predict how your system will react to certain situations in the future.

Fish Harvest

You may choose to harvest your fish all at once or in stages. If you do decide to harvest a majority of your fish, you will also want to harvest a majority of your plants. Removing fish from your system will reduce the amount of nitrogen significantly, which will cause stress for your plants.

Before you harvest your fish, make sure you can purchase new fry from a supplier. Some suppliers only have fry available during certain seasons, and you want to make sure your system is not running fishless for more than a few days.

Keep a log of when you harvest your fish and how many you harvested. This can affect water quality, and you will want this data for future planning.

Plant Harvest

Plants absorb many chemicals that would be toxic to fish. Therefore, you want to keep an even balance between the amount of fish in your tanks and the amount of plants in your grow beds.

Plant harvest happens more frequently than fish harvest, but plants are also easier to replace. Keep track of the time each plant will take from transplant to harvest, and start seeds so they are ready to replace old plants.

Keep track of which plants you have growing in your system, because different plants absorb nutrients at different rates. You may find that your fish do well when they are paired with leafy greens, but struggle when they are paired with fruiting vegetables. This may be due to a nutrient imbalance, and since there are so many factors that determine how well a system will function, your specific location may favor certain pairings over others.

Seed Starting

You will need to start seeds as you harvest old plants. Keep in mind how long seeds take to germinate and grow to a size suitable for transplant. For instance, you will want to start lettuce seeds 3 weeks before your harvest. Then, when you have harvested your heads of lettuce, the seedlings will be able to replace them.

Keep track of when you start your seeds, and how mature they were when you transplanted them. This will help you plan when to start your seeds in the future, and how each crop responds to transplanting. Experiment with different seed starting media if you are having trouble starting a certain vegetable.

Troubleshooting

Even the most meticulously-maintained system will have issues from time to time. Many problems can be fixed with small, gradual adjustments. Overcorrecting can result in larger problems that can cause significantly more damage.

There are 6 common problems with an aquaponic system:

- Nutrient deficiencies/toxicities
- Insects
- Disease
- Failure to fruit
- Dirty water
- Sick/stressed fish

Luckily, these problems are also easy to fix. A clean, balanced system that is within the proper nutrient, pH, and temperature ranges will rarely have an issue. However, it's important to know how to recognize these common issues and understand how to correct them.

Nutrient Deficiencies/Toxicities

The most common nutrient deficiencies in an aquaponic system are:

- Nitrogen
- Potassium
- Calcium
- Iron

Nitrogen, potassium, and iron deficiencies all result in yellow leaves. However, they discolor in different leaf structures, which can help you differentiate between them. Increase fish feed to increase nitrogen.

A nitrogen deficiency will result in a leaf that yellows from the tip of the leaf down towards the stem. It can also result in stunted plants with thin, wilted leaves.

A potassium deficiency will result in a leaf that has yellow veins with green leaf tissue. This will also cause poor flowering and fruit set. Potassium hydroxide and potassium carbonate will both increase potassium, but they will affect the pH differently, so it's important to do a pH test before adding a potassium amendment.

A calcium deficiency will result in a leaf that is curled up and dry. This will also cause poor fruit set and blossom end rot. Calcium carbonate and limestone will help increase calcium, but these will affect pH, so it's important to do a pH test before adding an amendment.

An iron deficiency will have yellow veins with yellow or white leaf tissue. Iron deficiency can mimic nitrogen deficiency, so it's important to know how a leaf responds to iron or nitrogen deficiencies in order to add the correct amendment. Chelated iron is the only suitable amendment for iron deficiencies.

Insects

Traditional vegetable gardens have a diverse ecosystem of beneficial insects that keep pests at bay. However, an aquaponic system is such a controlled environment that it cannot support a diverse population of beneficial bugs.

This can allow a pest problem to get out of hand very quickly, which means prompt response is absolutely necessary for pest problems.

The most common aquaponic insects are:

- Aphids
- Caterpillars
- Mealy bugs

There are also many crop-specific pests that may infest your plants, which is why it's important to research crops before you plant them. Aphids, caterpillars, and mealy bugs can infest any crop at any time, which is why you must know what they look like and how to treat them.

The problem with insect infestations is that many insecticides have wetting agents that are extremely toxic to fish. Therefore, if you see signs of aphids, caterpillars, or mealy bugs, it is best to throw out any infested plants and destroy them.

Aphids are small, light green bugs that feed on sap. Aphids will crowd around a leaf or flower base and leave a sticky residue.

schankz/Shutterstock.com

Caterpillars are easy to identify on plants, and they can do massive damage in a short amount of time. Large holes in leaves are the classic indicator of caterpillars.

MLHoward/Shutterstock.com

Mealy bugs are white, fuzzy, sticky insects that feed on the sap left behind by aphids. If an aphid infestation goes unchecked, a mealy bug infestation is sure to follow. Avoid mealy bugs by avoiding aphids, and destroy any infested plants before it can spread to your entire crop.

Noppharat7824/Shutterstock.com

Disease

Aquaponic plants are highly susceptible to rot, fungus, and mildew. These systems keep plants wet constantly, and also create a microclimate of high humidity, which encourages these diseases.

It is impossible to find a spray for these diseases that is harmless for fish. The most common cause of rot, fungus, and mildew is lack of ventilation and poor water circulation and quality. If you see signs of disease, do a water test and check your solids filter. If your water is sludgy, disease will follow.

Destroy any plants that show signs of disease, clean out your solids filter, and increase aeration. If you have media-filled beds, add red wiggler worms to your grow beds. Warm water temperatures can increase the risk of disease, so try to keep your water on the cooler end of what the fish will tolerate.

You may also have to drain off 1/3 of your system water and replace it with fresh water. Clean, balanced systems should not have a major issue with disease.

Failure to Fruit

This is a frustrating dilemma. Often, fruiting vegetables are beautiful, lush, and green. They simply refuse to flower or fruit.

This is generally caused by *too much* nitrogen. Nitrogen encourages leafy green growth, but too much will cause plants to focus on leaves instead of fruit. Try to reduce the amount of fish feed to lower nitrogen levels.

If your plants are indoors, they may not be getting the right light for fruiting. Grow lights with more blue wavelengths will encourage leaf growth, while grow lights with more red wavelengths will encourage flowers and fruit. If you are switching from leafy crops to fruiting crops, consider switching your grow lights for proper fruit set.

Dirty Water

If the water in your system is dirty, this can lead to disease for your plants and fish. Clean water is essential for a healthy system.

A properly-functioning solids filter is vital for clean water. Clean out your solids filter on a weekly basis until the water clears up. If you are using media-filled beds, consider adding red wiggler worms to help break down the solids in the sludge layer of your grow beds.

Warm temperatures combined with high nitrogen can result in an algae bloom. If your system has an algae bloom, it can clog pipes, restrict water movement, and absorb the nutrients intended for your crops.

If you notice algae in your system, try to limit the amount of light that reaches the water. Cover your fish tank and make sure your rafts reach the edges of your grow beds. Lower the temperature of your water (if possible) as far as you can while remaining within the healthy range for your fish.

If your water is still murky, try draining off 1/3 of the system water and replacing it with fresh water.

Sick/Stressed Fish

Dirty water, nutrient imbalances, and infested plants will result in stress for your fish. Stressed fish quickly become sick fish, and you can lose an entire fish tank if these issues are not addressed.

Signs that your fish are stressed include:

- Aggression
- Rubbing the sides of the tank
- Floating at the top of the tank (alive)
- Reduced appetite
- Reduced activity

If you notice your fish have changed their behavior, look back at your logs for temperature, water quality, and pH tests. Compare this with other issues your system may be having, such as root rot or aphids.

Adjust the temperature to the lower end of the ideal range for your species. Increase feeding rate to see how well they are eating, and increase aeration.

If this does not help, try removing fish to see if they respond to a lower stocking density. You should also clean out your solids filter and any buildup in your grow beds. You may also try a gradual change in fish feed to something more nutritious.

Maintaining an aquaponic system can be time-consuming, but it is also highly rewarding. Consistent testing, logging, and monitoring will help you anticipate and plan for potential issues. As you become more comfortable with your system, you will be able to tailor the maintenance schedule to your setup, and produce high-quality, nutritious vegetables year-round.

Once you have a healthy operation, you can begin to experiment with different design modifications, fish species, and crop varieties. Aquaponics is still an experimental field of agriculture, and new designs are constantly improving efficiency and productivity.

If in doubt; experiment. Once you are familiar with a basic system, you can experiment with different designs and crops, and you can tailor a design to your specific needs.

Aquaponic systems are versatile and enjoyable. They are easy to customize for any location and any purpose. With the ability to grow ten times the amount of healthy produce as a traditional garden, it's easy to see why these systems are gaining popularity.

As you research, plan, design, and build your system, remember that aquaponics is still an experimental growing method. Keep moving forward. Find what works best for your location, and make adjustments as you learn more about your system.

Enjoy the process, keep learning, and have fun!

About the Author

Richard's father was a keen gardener and that is where his interest in all natural things began. As a youngster, he enjoyed nothing better than helping his father in the garden.

Nowadays, he finds himself at the opposite end of life. Having had a satisfying career, he now has time to potter around in his garden and take care of his small homestead. Much of the food on his dinner table is homegrown. He likes to experiment with various gardening methods and find new ways to grow bountiful crops year-round.

He wants to share his knowledge and show how easy and rewarding it is to set up your own prosperous garden. In his opinion, you don't need a huge budget to get started. When you do get started, you will soon feel, and taste, the benefits of growing your own food.

Learn more about Richard Bray at *amazon.com/author/richardbray*

Printed in Great Britain
by Amazon

26739409R00108